# Studies in
# The Elizabethan Theatre

Edited by

## CHARLES T. PROUTY

*Professor of English, Yale University*

1961

THE SHOE STRING PRESS, INC.

Library of Congress Catalogue Card No: 61-9877
Printed in the United States of America

CONTENTS

# CONTENTS

# INTRODUCTION

Nowadays Shakespeare is much in the news: his plays are currently to be presented by a professional company in the schools of New York; Shakespeare Festivals multiply apace; and the American Shakespeare Festival Theatre has its first nation-wide tour in progress. In the paperback book market editions of the plays and books about them find a willing market. Finally, television has brought several of the plays to their largest audience in history.

In a purely dramatic sense current interest in the physical aspects of theatre should have some connection with modern Shakespearean production. Off-Broadway has theatres in the round, a sandwich theatre with the audience on either side of the stage, and many other departures from the standard proscenium arch stage. Critics such as Brooks Atkinson and several playwrights have expressed their dissatisfaction with the proscenium stage and their desire to escape from the familiar three-sided room thus presented. At Stratford, Ontario, the plays are seen in a fascinating kind of amphitheatre with the spectators seated in rising tiers so that they almost surround and look down on the "tongue" stage.

Students of theatre history are well aware that the modern proscenium stage is a direct descendant of the Restoration stage. Very simply, the great public theatres of Elizabethan and Stuart times had been closed in 1642 and being of no use had been demolished. The Court returning from exile in France brought with it the French theatre based on the "tennis court" theatres. Basically this was a narrow rectangular hall with a picture frame which could be closed by a curtain. Thus the Medieval and Renaissance tradition of staging disappeared and a new tradition was established which resulted in the realistic three-sided room so carefully described in every detail by Ibsen. Today the desire is to escape from such rigid conventions, but if we are to go back to an earlier form of stage or theatre we must begin with some factual knowledge of what that stage was like and what its conventions were.

At the various Festivals and in dramatic museums models of the famous Globe playhouse are on exhibition, but a comparison of these models shows interesting variations in external shape, details of architecture, and in the stage itself. The plain fact of the matter is that we have no exact factual knowledge of the Globe. We do know, however, the contract for the building of the Fortune Theatre in 1599 and that contract twice mentions the Globe. Peter Streete, the building contractor, had only recently undertaken the demolition of the Theatre, the first home of Shakespeare's company, the Lord Chamberlain's Men, and had transported the materials to the South bank where he had erected the Globe. The Fortune, according to the contract was rectangular, but the Globe was either round or polygonal, so the dimensions of the former tell us nothing about the Globe. In speaking of the stairs, passageways (Conveyances), and divisions of the galleries, the Fortune contract says that these are to be "as are made & contryved in and to the late erected Plaiehowse on the Banck in the saide parishe of $S^{te}$ Saviours called the Globe." After specifying the length (Fortie and Three foote of lawfull assize), and the breadth (to extende to the middle of the yarde of the saide howse) and other details of the stage, the contract continues, "and the saide Stadge to be in all other proporcions contryved and fashioned like vnto the Stadge of the Saide Plaie howse called the Globe." These two references plus the rather uncertain evidence of several views of London constitute all the specific knowledge that we have concerning the "Globe Plaiehowse." Thus all we can say about the Globe is that it had a platform stage surrounded on three sides by spectators who stood in the pit or sat in the galleries.

Two familiar features of practically all reconstructions are an inner stage curtained off and an upper stage. There is no mention of these areas in the Fortune contract, but they have been postulated upon certain details in the plays of Shakespeare and other Elizabethans. In about one half of the plays of Shakespeare the action calls for some kind of a raised or upper playing area and/or an area enclosed by curtains. A complicating factor in any recreation of these areas is generally overlooked and that is the fact that plays were presented in a great variety of places. For example, plays from the public theatres were presented at Court. Various precepts of the City of London authorities show that the players used inns, gaming houses, taverns, halls, breweries, mansion houses, courts, gardens, orchards and other places. As late as 1601 "open streets and houses" were used for forty performances of Richard II according to the direct statement of Queen Elizabeth herself. Using such a variety of locales the players had, of necessity, to be extremely flexible in matters of production.

While the scholar knows something about the conditions of dramatic production in the Elizabethan age, very little knowledge of this finds its way into the schools and colleges and less into the non-academic world. An example may be seen in modern productions of Shakespeare and the occasional revival of other Elizabethan playwrights. Even when a platform stage is used without a curtain there are innumerable "blackouts" which substitute for the fall of a curtain in a conventional theatre and so stop the flow of the play. There is no authority for these in the original texts and physically it would have been impossible given the circumstances of production in various open-air playing areas.

Two great principles underlie all Elizabethan staging: the first is the platform stage, a neutral playing area that can be transformed by the entry of "Serving men ... with their napkins" from a street in Verona to the great hall of Capulet's house. Romeo, Mercutio, Benvolio and others never leave the stage; the action flows on and the platform stage has changed the scene by the simple device of the servingmen. This episode illustrates the second principle of production: there is no break in action. The long text of Hamlet can be presented in approximately three and one-half hours if these two principles are observed. "Blackouts" or falling curtains destroy continuity and lengthen the time of performance. A recent Othello, a relatively short play, required three full hours with but one intermission.

If the stage was a simple platform, other details of production were not. During the past summer a very fine production of The Tempest was presented at Stratford, Connecticut. Shakespeare's poetry was allowed to set the scene; there was no revolving rock; and no Prospero's cell; but the masques were presented with elaborate costumes, dance, and music. There was general praise of the production, but a number of people objected to the masques as being un-Elizabethan. A reading of Mr. Paterson's account of the Revels Office demonstrates beyond question that there was almost no limit to the luxury and variety of costumes produced by this Office for entertainment at Court.

Most graduate students have heard of the Office of the Revels but very few have examined the manifold details of the accounts so carefully and laboriously transcribed by Professor Feuillerat. It comes as a surprise to most to discover how sophisticated and elaborate Court productions were. Elizabethan plays were filled with colour in both costumes and properties but again the gap between the scholar's knowledge and that of the average college graduate has hitherto been unbridged.

Even more remote is knowledge today of the first private theatre opened in London the same year as the first public playhouse, "The Theatre," which was built by James Burbage with the financial assistance of his brother-in-law, John Brayne. Nowadays there are few undergraduate courses in Elizabethan Drama where the plays of Greene, Peele, Marlowe, and John Lyly are read, but the last named was the great purveyor of plays for the Court during the 1580's. From Campaspe in 1584? to Midas 1590?, Lyly's plays were presented at Court while both Campaspe and Sapho and Phao contain

two prologues: one for Court, and the other for performance at the Blackfriar's. The actors in all of Lyly's plays
were children regularly employed as choristers while
others were students in schools. Just what kind of theatre
existed in the buildings which had been a conventual establishment was unknown until the discoveries of Professors
Feuillerat and Wallace in the early years of the century.
While we now have some knowledge of the physical aspects
of this "private" theatre, we desire to know a great deal
more, but two things are clear: performances were given
in an enclosed area where artificial light was needed and
before a very small audience – in comparison with the
2,000 or 2,500 of The Theatre. Obviously, a higher admission price could be demanded and the beginnings of
a coterie as opposed to a public audience are clear. The
sophisticated, presumably courtly, audience was given
plays not seen in the public theatre and this kind of play
affected the subsequent development of Elizabethan and
Jacobean Drama as Professor Harbage has so well
demonstrated in his book Shakespeare and the Rival
Traditions. Mr. Sarlos' survey of this theatre and the
companies of children who acted there follows the principles of the other essays in bringing together what we do
know and what problems still remain.

   It is no wonder in this age of specialization, and in
the critical milieu in which plays are studied, not as plays
that reach fruition only in actual performance, but as
literature or poetry to be examined on the printed page
that the undergraduate, the graduate student, and the
teacher have no great awareness of the matters here discussed. It is the aim of this book, therefore, to present
a brief synthesis of three aspects of Elizabethan theatre
that will make the reading and seeing on stage of the
plays of Shakespeare and his contemporaries more under-
standable and more rewarding.

# THE STAGECRAFT OF THE REVELS OFFICE
## DURING THE REIGN OF ELIZABETH

### as Suggested by
### Documents Relating to the Office

by

Morton Paterson

# INTRODUCTION

The Documents relating to the Office of the Revels in the time of Queen Elizabeth, edited by Albert Feuillerat in 1910, consists of instructions, charts, letters, grants, expenses and others records collected and kept by the Revels Office during the years 1555-1589. Feuillerat's edition corrects earlier interpretations of Cunningham and Collier. As Feuillerat states (Documents 1908: xi), [1] "It was urgent, therefore, that somebody should dispel the mist of suspicion which has for long paralyzed the efforts of many scholars, when it has not led them into dangerous pitfalls." The Documents provide invaluable information about the history, administration and theatrical craft of the Revels Office. The first two, history and administration, have been thoroughly treated by Chambers in The Elizabethan Stage and to a lesser extent by Feuillerat in Le Bureau des Menus Plaisirs. Both of these authors treat also of the stagecraft of the office, but not in exhaustive or conveniently organized ways. A complete treatment of Elizabethan staging in general or even of Elizabethan court staging would involve much more research than the present writer intended. Therefore, the purpose of the present paper is to compile and organize the information in the Revels Documents relevant to stage practice. This organization should be useful to students of Renaissance literature interested in the theatrical aspect of Court drama. To help the general reader or any student unfamiliar with the Revels Office, a summary of the general nature and function of the office has been given in Section I. Historians of the theater are probably already acquainted with most of the factual information presented in the Revels accounts but may be nevertheless interested in some of the general conclusions reached.

The importance of any detail in the documents can be suggested only through a general knowledge of Elizabethan stage practice. Therefore, general works on the Elizabethan and Renaissance stage have been consulted for aid

in interpreting the facts found in the accounts. The main
import of the present paper is the surprising opulence
with which the Revels productions were staged. In addition, the particularly Elizabethan style of such opulence
should be made clear in the following pages. Finally, the
ageless devices of theatrical artifice used by the Revels
should be of interest. The Revels Documents present a
humane as well as an artistic subject.

# I. PURPOSE OF THE OFFICE

To the Elizabethans "revels" meant theatrical entertainment at Court. The Revels Office was the department
of the royal household in charge of furnishing that entertainment. The functions of the office, denominated in
brief "the Revels," stemmed from the need to provide
diversion for the Court at medieval Christmas celebra-
tions. In the fifteenth century the Office of Tents, which
supplied equipment for tournaments, and the Office of the
Wardrobe, which furnished stuffs and clothing for the
Queen, were capable of devising the accessories and costumes necessary for theatrical performances. The need
for a separate Revels Office resulted largely from the
greater interest shown by Henry VIII in court entertainment. At the beginning of Elizabeth's reign, in 1559, to be
exact, the Revels was finally established as an independent
office. The general nature of the task of the office is expressed at various places in the accounts. The most succinct statement is the following (Documents 1908: 129):

> . . the Apparelling, Disgyzing, ffurnishing,
> ffitting Garnishing & orderly setting foorthe
> of men, women, & Children: in sundry
> Tragedies, Playes, Maskes and sportes
> with their apte howses of paynted Canvas &
> properties incident suche as mighte most
> lyvely expresse the effect of the histories
> plaied & Devises in Maskes this yeare
> showen at the Coorte for her Maiesties
> Regall Disporte & Recreation . .

Such activities were carried on during the entire reign of
Elizabeth.

Four officers were appointed to the Revels. The
Master was usually a gentleman, sometimes of high rank,
responsible to the Lord Chamberlain. His job was, on
the one hand, to be aware of the prevailing interests and
tastes of the Court and, on the other hand, to hire and

co-ordinate the players and artisans who could give the
Court the most satisfying entertainment.  His work resembled in many ways the tasks of a modern theatrical
producer, who selects a play, a director, scene designer,
costumer and other members of a production staff.  The
second officer was the Yeoman, who supervised directly
the many workmen employed by the office.  He was frequently a master tailor and occasionally had served in the
Office of the Wardrobe.  The two other officers were
clerks responsible for keeping records of supplies on
hand, new supplies, piecework, wages and other expenses.
All the officers, in addition to wages and privileges accru-
ing to their offices, were given lodging in the hospital of
St. John of Jerusalem, in Blackfriars, where the workrooms of the Revels were located.

The types of entertainment selected by the Master
were most frequently masks and plays.  Masks were
basically semi-dramatic dances performed by amateurs,
usually ladies and gentlemen of the Court.  Speeches,
which often accompanied or interrupted the dancing, were
usually given by a non-participating spokesman, a kind of
dramatic master of ceremonies, called a trunchman.
There were other speaking parts, however, as the quotation below will indicate.  The entrance of the maskers,
who wore costumes and face-masks, created an element
of surprise.  Only those participants in the mask who
came into the room from outside—that is, from the street
or from another room—wore masks.  That such was the
usual Elizabethan practice is shown by the masks in Act I,
scene 4, of Romeo and Juliet and Act II, scene 1, of Much
Ado About Nothing.  The stage directions of these scenes
indicate face-masks only for those entering from outside.
The performers produced a pleasing climax to the mask
by dancing with the more important members of the audience.  The following is the most complete single statement in the accounts of the dramatic nature of a mask.
Actually a prelude to a mask, rather than the main body of
action, is probably being described (Documents 1908:  146):

6

> . . one of the forenamed Maskes had going
> before it A childe gorgeously decked for
> Mercury, who uttered A speeche: and pre-
> sented iiii fflowers (wroughte in silke and
> golde) to the Queenes Maiestie signefieing,
> peace and plenty to ensue. He had also ii
> torchebearers . . with him.

Except for an account of sound effects involved in a hunting scene (Documents 1908: 141), the action of other
masks must be derived from scattered and uncertain items
in the Revels accounts.

The histories, tragedies and comedies presented at
Court during the years 1559 to 1589 were drawn from the
repertories of and presented by the following companies:

| Noblemen's Troups | Boys' Troups |
|---|---|
| Sir Robert Lane | Westminster |
| Earl of Leicester | St. Paul |
| Lord Clinton | Windsor |
| Lord Howard | The Chapel |
| Earl of Warwick | Earl of Oxford |
| Earl of Derby | Merchant Tailors |
| Lord Hudson | |
| Lord Strange | The Inns |
| The Queen | |
| Lord Admiral | Gray's Inn |
| Lord Chamberlain | |

Other Troups

Italian Players
Symon and his Fellows

Tumblers are also mentioned in the accounts; no doubt,
other kinds of entertainers also appeared at Court.

Unfortunately the accounts make little distinction between masks and plays. In masks the usual scenic interest, aside from the dancing, was largely that of costumes
and their scenic grouping. On a typical theatrical evening,

7

which might last from ten o'clock to one in the morning,
the mask was performed after the play, and so adapted
itself to the scenery already used or else ignored it. Ex-
ceptions occur, of course. For example, the mask presented by Elizabeth in 1572 –her most lavish theatrical
display –for the visiting Duc de Montmorency was fully
staged with scenery, properties and special effects. However, that masks could be produced with little besides
costumes is shown in the listing of expenses for a mask
sent to Scotland in 1589: costumes for maskers and torchbearers are all that are mentioned (Documents 1908: 392).
The stage houses frequently mentioned in the accounts are
always associated with players rather than maskers. The
pageant cars used in the masks were, of course, mobile
and could be wheeled onto the stage or among the audience
without disturbing the stationary scenery used for the
plays. (For a description of stage houses and pageant cars
see the sections below on Scenery and Properties.) Contemporary accounts of Elizabethan masks and the texts of
the plays offer a better means of defining the scenic nature
of the two genres than does the information in the Revels
accounts.


## II.  THE PRODUCTION SCHEDULE

Elizabeth returned to hold Court in the fall. Soon
after, the nature and number of shows for the approaching
season were determined according to her wishes by the
Master of the Revels and the Lord Chamberlain. The first
duty of the Master was to call together the available companies of actors for the performing or reciting of their
repertory. The auditions took place in the great hall of
St. John's or in the lodgings of the Master (Chambers
1923: I, 86). Evidently the try-outs were elaborate,
since cumbersome properties as well as the services of
musicians were brought in for them. After the best plays
were chosen by the Master, it was within his discretion

to make changes in them, either by deletions, slight changes or the insertion of specially written new scenes (Chambers 1923: I, 224; Documents 1908: 145). The designers were then put to work on patterns and models for the costumes, certain properties and scenery. The Revels workmen began work ordinarily around the last of October. The Master had power to requisition the following workmen: tailors, painters, embroiderers, haberdashers, propertymakers, hatters, carders, joiners, glaziers, armorers, basket-makers, furriers, sadlers, plasterers, plumemakers and wheelwrights (Documents 1908: 51). The number of workmen employed, of which tailors, painters and embroiders constituted the large majority, might rise as high as one hundred eight (in 1573) or drop to twelve (in 1587-1588); the average was fifty (Feuillerat 1910: 56). Work was thus begun for the first production, which was usually given on Christmas or a day or two afterwards.

The time spent by the tailors in preparation for the productions might exceed the two months time from October to Christmas. For the six masks and six plays given during the season of 1571-72 and for the three masks and eight plays of 1572-73, a score (Documents 1908: 12)[2] of tailors worked, for each season, on the average of eighty days and seventeen nights. Since a Revels workday was ten hours and a worknight six hours (Documents 1908: 12), the total just quoted would equal about a hundred thirteen modern working days. For these same seasons an average of nine embroiderers, haberdashers and propertymakers – including carpenters and joiners – worked about seventy-five modern working days. The Master, who was on hand during the whole time of preparation, received four shillings a day; the Yeoman and the two clerks, also present, were paid two shillings a day. Tailors got a shilling, propertymakers eighteen pence (Documents 1908: passim).[3] For a single mask given in May of 1559 an average of ten tailors worked for twelve days, while four painters worked for five days (Documents 1908: 97). This amount of time and work might be taken as the average time

9

required for the preparation of a single show. The work-time for twelve shows given in 1571 was, accordingly, about twelve times as great. Large departures from the average did occur, however.

After the costumes, properties and scenery were constructed, they were transported by barge or cart from the workrooms to the Court. The Office of Works by this time had probably finished putting up a stage in the great hall of one of the winter palaces. Westminster, Hampton Court, Richmond, Greenwich, Windsor and Whitehall were frequently used. The construction work involved in the erection of a stage was evidently too heavy for the Revels Office and proper to that of the Works. The Revels carpenters had only to set up on the stage the scenery for the first play and to store the costumes and properties in some adjacent room.

One excerpt from the accounts of the Office of Works will give an idea of what that office was responsible for as well as a description of one of the stages its workmen erected (quoted in Hotson 1954: 69-70):

> Framing postes and Railes for plaies,
> setting up degrees in the great chamber,
> nailinge on Brackettes & boorders for
> the people to sett on, makeing new Hal-
> paces there for the Queens Majesties use,
> and a newe stage of xiiii foote square for
> the Plaiers to plaie on, and Halpaces for
> the Lordes and Ladies to sett on, and iii
> other Halpaces for the people to stand on.

We need not assume that all court stages were only fourteen feet square.

The great hall of a royal palace measured on the average 40 by 105 feet. The great hall at Whitehall was 45 feet wide and about 100 feet long (Chambers 1923: I, 15). Across one end of the hall was a screen-wall containing two service doors. The stage was probably set in front of it so that the players could make use of the space behind the doors as a "[re]tiring room." In front of the stage was probably an area of floor space used by dancers in the masks; and at the nonstage edge of the dance space the Queen's "state" or dias was usually placed. A musicians' loft was commonly erected along one of the side walls (Hotson 1954: 136). Wooden tiers of seats for the ladies and gentlemen of the court and some standing-room tiers for the people lined the side walls and filled much of the space behind the dias. Space was left in the tiers along a side wall or the rear wall for passage to the hall's main door, at which some of the Queen's guard were usually stationed (Hotson 1954: 136).

The following is a schedule of the productions of one of the busier theatrical seasons, 1573-74:

| Day | Place | Plays and masks | Actors |
|------|-------|-----------------|--------|
| Nov. ? | Greenwich | A mask | ? |
| Dec. 26 | Whitehall | Predor and Lucia | Leicester's |
| Dec. 27 | Whitehall | Alkmeon Lanceknights mask | St. Paul's |
| Dec. 28 | Whitehall | Mamillia | Leicester's |
| Jan. 1 | Whitehall | Triumph of Truth, etc. Forresters mask | Westminster's |
| Jan. 3 | Whitehall | Herpetulus | Clinton's |
| Jan. 6 | Whitehall | Quintus Fabius Sages mask | Windsor's |
| Feb. 2 | Hampton Ct. | Timoclia at Thebes | Merchant Tailors' |
| Shrove Mon. ? | Hampton Ct. | Virtuous ladies Philemon and Felicia | Leicester's |
| Tues. ? | Hampton Ct. | Percius and Anthominis Warriors mask Ladies mask | Merchant Tailors' |
| July ? | Windsor | Pastime | Italian Players |
| July ? | Reading | A pastoral | Italian Players |

The number of productions per season varied from as few as three in 1563-64 to as many as sixteen in 1573-74. The average number per season was eight. During the summer progresses of the Queen entertainment was furnished her by the noblemen she visited, at their expense. The Revels Office did occasionally supplant the local entertainment, however, as is shown by the mention above of the Italian players appearing at Windsor and Reading. The lavish mask given for Montmorency, mentioned above, was given during the summer. To summarize the preceding information, we may say, while emphasizing wide departures, that on the average each year fifty workmen worked for two months to prepare eight shows for a theatrical season lasting from Christmas to Lent.

Costs varied considerably.[4] The single mask for Montmorency, which required the services of large numbers of workmen, some for as many as thirty days, cost a thousand pounds. It was given in a banquet house[5] erected by the Revels which cost two hundred thirty pounds. The total cost of the wages and materials required for a single mask in 1558 was about fifty pounds. In 1573-74 the charges of one play and one mask amounted to sixty-four pounds. Yet, in 1576 three plays and one mask cost together sixty-pounds. The average cost of each of the twelve shows given in 1571 could be roughly computed as one hundred twenty-three pounds. The foregoing figures mean that the cost of one show—it is useless to try to distinguish between plays and masks—was anywhere from fifteen to a hundred twenty-three pounds. The average cost, if such in reality could be said to exist, was, therefore, about thirty-five pounds. The total costs of each season are more definite. From 1560 to 1572 the yearly cost was never less than three hundred pounds and usually over five hundred. From 1572 until 1592 it was generally lower, around two hundred and fifty. The peak was Montmorency's visit, when costs rose to a total of one thousand five hundred eighty-five pounds. Alencon's visit during 1581-82 occasioned expenses of six hundred thirty pounds.

The average expenditure was about three hundred pounds per year. This figure nearly corresponds with the figures determined above of an average of eight shows per season at an average of thirty-five pounds each.

After each show the scenery, properties and costumes were returned to St. John's and stored. They remained there until the spring when the storeroom was put in order. We read of charges for the following in almost all the seasonal divisions of the accounts (Documents 1908: 102):

> Eyringe, repayringe, lainge abroode,
> turninge, sowinge, mendinge, tackinge,
> Spunginge, wypinge, brushinge, makinge
> cleane, foldinge and lainge up of the Maskes,
> garments, vesturs and other Stuffe, Store
> and Implements of the office for the Safegarde
> and refresshinge of same.

This work usually took about thirty-five days. Except for occasional summer entertainment, then, the Revels officers could rest until the following October, when work began for the following season.

## III. COSTUMES

Making costumes was the most important task of the Revels Office. The importance of costumes is shown in part by the fact that the Yeoman of the Revels was frequently also a master tailor and a former employee of the Wardrobe Office. As has been mentioned in Section I above, there was a long standing association between the Revels and the Wardrobe, such that one of the earlier Masters of the Revels, one Richard Gibson (Feuillerat 1910: 21), had been in charge of both offices.[6] During Elizabeth's reign the increased amount of activities of both offices made necessary the appointment of a separate master for each.

13

## Richness

It would be difficult to overestimate the richness and elaborateness of Renaissance stage costumes. First of all, the most expensive materials were used. This is not true today, when artificial fabrics, such as rayons and fake velvets, often serve. The Revels Office used large quantities of velvet, sarsenet, satin, damask, taffeta, caffa, baudekin (or baldachin) and cloth of gold and silver. These stuffs were not specially or sparingly used but furnished most of the costumes for all the masks and many plays. Many of the costumes included long or full garments which required several yards of material. A pair of sleeves for a torchbearer, for example, could take five yards of purple cloth of gold (Documents 1908: 34), and a pair of breeches could take seven yards of velvet (Norris 1938: 648).[7] The rich materials used by the office could be supplied in a great variety of colors by the Office of the Wardrobe. Satin, for example, could be had in plain colors of red, purple, crimson, incarnate (flesh), yellow, green, russet, murrey, black, white, blue and tawny. With figures it came in crimson with gold works (raised patterns), incarnate with gold works, black striped with gold, blue with gold threads striped with yellow, and in other colored stripes. The average price of satin was thirteen shillings per yard. Both silver and gold cloths came pure, mixed with threads of green, white, red, orange, crimson, black and other colors or raised with patterns. Mixed or raised cloths of gold cost sixteen shillings per yard; silver cost eight shillings (Documents 1908: passim)[8]. Tinsel, which was silk interwoven with gold or silver thread, came in red, black, tawny, blue-crimson, white, blue, russet, and purple or in raised patterns of black, purple and green. It cost ten shillings per yard. Velvet, one of the most used materials, which cost sixteen or seventeen shillings per yard, came in as many colors as the satin mentioned above. Taffeta, sarsenet and damask were also available in almost as many different colors. Such a source of materials is more plentiful by far than that drawn upon by most modern repertory theaters.

Aside from the rich stuffs just mentioned, other materials were used. Cendal (a sarsenet-like cloth) is listed, as well as chamlets ( a mohair, wool and silk fabric), flannel, lawn and tawny ( a woolen cloth of tawny color). Of the furs, wolverine, coon, lamb, kid and calf appear. Leather was also used. Of the cheaper cloths, felts and sackcloth, as well as a great deal of buckrams of all sorts, fustian cotton and canvas were extensively used. Raw silk or raw satin-silk was used to make artificial hair. The silk, in the case of beards, was often attached to a mask or vizard. One such mask was made to represent an ape (Documents 1908: 175). The silk was curled for use in a periwig of Xerxes (Documents 1908: 244). Beards are described as long, black and red, long white, and marquisotted. Horse and cow tails were used, but apparently for "wild mens garments" rather than for beards or wigs (Documents 1908: 227). Surprisingly, there is one instance of a costume partly made out of simple paper (Documents 1908: 308).

The costumes were not only rich but ornate. As has been said, much of the cloth, such as baudekin, brocade, damask and others, was decorated with figures, or works. Costumes were commonly decorated with fringes and borders. Borders, which are designated "gards" in the accounts, were often richly embroidered. There is mention of one border of red dornixe (a woolen cloth from Tournay, Belgium) embroidered with gold cloth and silver thread (Documents 1908: 99). Fringes were made of such rich materials as gold and silk. A list of other applied ornaments will give an idea of their variety: chevrons, flowers of silk, needle-work flowers, bells, spangles, buckles, feathers, tufts, bows, tassels, buttons (large, copper-silver, silk, green-gold, etc.), lace of various kinds, nets, stripes, braid, ribbons, counterfeit stones (rubies, pearls, sitterines, topazes), ornamental coins and pipes (a kind of gold or silver trimming). In addition

15

to these, aiglets, or eyelets, were arranged on the fronts
of many of the costumes. Aiglets were button-loops or
ties; they were mostly ornamental, being profusely used,
and were often tagged: that is, to the hanging ends of the
ties were attached metal tips or tags. When used on court
or street costumes the tags were often finely worked. All
the above ornaments give evidence that the stage costumes,
although probably not as finely sewn as street wear, were
equally elaborate. Indeed, there is evidence in the accounts that Revels costumes were worn by people of rank
at weddings and other non-theatrical occasions outside the
Court (Documents 1908:  409-10).[9] Such a custom shows
both that the costumes were well enough made to pass in
society and that some elements of society were themselves
of a rather theatrical nature.

Other methods were used to make costumes, both
street and stage, more sumptuous. One process, called
pinking, consisted in making small holes or slits in a garment in the form of a pattern. The contrastingly colored
lining shone through the holes. Another method was called
"pulling out," whereby the lining of a garment was drawn
through holes or slits in the outer material to produce
puffs. "Paning" was the application of parallel ribbon-
like strips of cloth set close together on the base material
of breeches, bodices or sleeves. The considerable amount
of work involved in these processes explains the frequent
references in the accounts to sums paid to individual workmen for the pinking and paning of various garments. Certainly, the finery of court dress of the time was matched
in the elaborate and sumptuous costumes created by the
Revels Office.

Historical Accuracy

The depiction of contemporary dress on the stage
raises the question of historical and geographical accuracy.
The designers who worked for the Revels were certainly
capable of distinguishing the national costumes of the
times. The skin of Moors, for example, was reproduced

by covering the actor's arms and legs with black velvet.
Their supposed curly hair was imitated by the use of black
lambskins. According to Feuillerat (Feuillerat 1910: 58),
the Allmaynes (Germans) who appeared in an early mask
of Elizabeth's reign were quite recognizable. They wore
doublets of gold cloth with large full sleeves of crimson
and incarnate velvet, slashed and denticulated, lined with
yellow sarsenet, and edged with narrow fringes of silver.
Their trunk hose, or breeches, were of the same velvet,
full (i. e., like slops) and also slashed and denticulated.
Such was the costume of German mercenaries at the time.
The scant knowledge of classical or ancient dress is shown
by a description in the accounts of the costume of an Acteon.
The contemporary nature of his costume may conveniently
be seen by comparing an itemization of it with that of the
dress of one Herr Breuning, a Dutchman who bought a new
suit of clothes for a projected trip to the English Court
in 1595:

| Acteon (Documents 1908: 38) | | Herr Breuning (Norris 1938: 648) | |
|---|---|---|---|
| hunting cloak | – black-gold tinsel | cloth for a cloak | – ? |
| slops | – purple gold | breeches | – velvet |
| jerkin | – purple gold | doublet | – velvet ? |
| long buskins with copper buttons | – orange velvet | silk hose three dozen buttons | – silk |
| gold and Paris silk linings | | gold braid and lace linings | |
| headpiece | | fustian and other stuffs | |
| wooden spears | | | |

The correspondence is not perfect, but in the essential
items of cloak, doublet and breeches contemporary style
is evident. It would appear that in the case of the Acteon
the colors have been brightened and exaggerated; and, of
course, a fanciful headdress and a spear have been added.
Buskins were a traditional item in Elizabethan stage and
street dress, though they were probably not classical in

17

form. The leaves on the lining and headpiece probably
indicated a kind of camouflage and as such were probably
the only accurate element in the hunter's costume. The
effect of a similarly unrealistic combination may be seen
in a picture of a mask of the time wherein a boy angel is
represented (Wickham 1959: I, plate XXI). He wears
wings on his back, but the rest of the costume is the usual
jerkin and breeches. Thus, historical and supernatural
variations from the contemporary norm were purely fanciful. In the case of intentionally contemporary costumes,
such as those of the Allmaynes mentioned above, the colors
and materials were theatricalized. The mariners in a
Mask of Mariners, for example, wore jerkins, slops and
hoods; but the garments were made of purple-gold, blue-
gold and green-silver materials.

A favorite type of costume, and one which strikes a
kind of exotic and historical middle ground, was that of the
ornamental gown. Gowns were worn by the Elizabethans,
particularly by the professional classes; however, in color-
ful and perhaps gaudy form they were used to costume
such characters as Barbarians, Turkish magistrates, and
Venetian senators. The gown was generally loose, long
and richly decorated with borders, stripes, flowers,
fringes and other ornaments. The sleeves, made of the
same material as the gown, hung low at the wrist, thereby revealing close-fitting undersleeves of a contrasting
color. That such gowns, in their general form at least,
held little precise significance is shown by the fact that an
ordinary torchbearer might also wear one. The main
interest of the Revels officers was evidently the production
of as rich costumes as possible. Even Irish kerns, whose
poverty at the time was proverbial (Feuillerat 1910: 58),
were costumed in shirts of yellow sarsenet and tunics of
gold-crimson cloth with fringes of green silk.

The women's costumes were contemporary and hence
anachronistic, in many cases, in the same way as the
men's costumes. Diana, for example, was costumed in
"glove sleeves" and vague garments designated "upper,

18

nether and long." She wore the contemporary partlet (a
white covering of the upper chest) and a girdle (a belt
with pendant ends). Diana's nymphs are dressed in the
standard kirtle of the day—a bodice and skirt combination
that leaves little skin exposed. Without appearing dis-
crepant, the women, like the men, could wear theatrical
headpieces.

There are three articles of dress, two of them mentioned above, which constitute a distinctive aspect of
Elizabethan costuming and so deserve special mention:
headpieces, buskins and gloves. It is tempting but difficult to derive the nature of the theatrical headpieces from
the descriptions given in the accounts. Contemporary
feminine court dress included a variety of headdresses,
but these do not appear to have been large or fancy enough
to fit descriptions of theatrical headgear given in the accounts. Perhaps the general shape of the larger types of
court headdress served as a model for stage types. The
book Costume and Fashion (Norris 1938: 744) shows a
woman wearing a headdress consisting of a fairly close
fitting, coif-like covering for the forepart of the head, with
a decorative border called a billiment framing the fore-
head and a curtain-like piece of cloth hanging from a small
frame at the back of the head. The hanging piece separated
at the shoulders. That some sort of sturdy frame was required for the theatrical headpieces is shown by the many
allusions in the accounts to sums paid to the basketmaker
for the construction of wicker headpieces (Documents 1908:
80-82). The headpiece was sometimes specially designed
in a sketch or pattern (Documents 1908: 177) and was made
of such rich materials as tissue gold (cloth of twisted gold
and silk threads) and red velvet. Ornamentation, which
was profuse, included, in addition to billiments, festoons
of various sorts, tufts of feathers, plumes, counterfeit
stones, and spangles. Single and double headpieces are
mentioned, as well as a headpiece with "compartments."
It is possible that the standard theatrical headdress was
similar to the tall conical hats worn by women in the late

19

fifteenth century. Such hats were called hennins and included long pendant bunches of cloth held over the back of the head. However traditional, the headpiece must have constituted an important part of stage dress, particularly in the masks, and was evidently an elaborate, if not a towering, construction. Unfortunately, information in the accounts is not particular about their size and shape.

Leslie Hotson sheds a great deal of light on the head-pieces, or "tires," as they were called. He writes (Hotson 1949: 174-179):

> Actually, their head-dresses were marvellous confections of gold, pearl, and precious stones. The foundation was a coif, caul, hair-net, or hair-lace cunningly woven of gold thread, in or on which jewels were mounted. One of Queen Elizabeth's tires was "a Jewel, being a ship of Mother-of-Pearl, garnished with rubies." And in Montemayor's Diana we have this: "The attyre of her head was in the form of two little ships made of emeralds, with all the shrouds and tackling made of clear saphyres."

Hotson adds that the "tire-maker's and wire-drawer's art came to France and England from Venice" and quotes Falstaff's remark to Mistress Ford: "Thou hast the right arched beauty of the brow that becomes the ship-tire, the tire valiant, or any tire of Venetian admittance." Hotson quotes also a canzonet of Thomas Morley which is illuminating:

> In nets of golden wires,
> With pearl and ruby spangled,
> My heart entangled
> Cries out and help requires.

The wicker and wire which the Revels accounts indicate were used would indeed allow the construction of very large headpieces.

The buskinmaker was an artisan often employed by

the Revels office. Buskins, or stertops as they were
sometimes called, were soft, fairly close-fitting, boot-
like socks which usually reached to below the knee where
the tops were turned down. They were worn with contemporary dress for protection during travel. Theatrical
buskins were generally less substantial and of fancier
materials. Taffeta, velvet, satin and cloth of gold and
silver were used. Some were buttoned (Documents 1908:
177), others were laced with ribbon (Documents 1908: 159).
The soles were of leather (Documents 1908: 177). That
stage buskins were bright, if not gaudy, is shown by the
case of the Acteon, mentioned above, who wore long buskins of orange velvet fitted with copper buttons. Again,
Renaissance ideas of classical dress and even of classical
dress in functional contemporary form were always subject to fancy.

Almost all the actors, maskers and torchbearers
wore gloves. The glovemakers employed by the Revels
continually received orders for a dozen or so pairs.
Torchbearers were perhaps glad to protect their hands
from dripping candlewax or torch oil, but the major value
seems to have been one of style. Gloves were, of course,
a common form of gift in the sixteenth century. The mention in the accounts (Documents 1908: 380) reading

> ffor gloves geven to the Queenes players to
> ye tumblers & children of Poles . . . xxxvjs

may mean that the gloves mentioned were intended as a
permanent gift. Gloves are designated in the accounts as
"fine," "coarse," "cut," "of calves leather," "Spanish,"
"very good washed," "for the ladies," and "pointed."
Points were a kind of thread-lace made by the needle.
Court gloves of the period were often made with large embroidered gauntlets covering the wrist and as such could
be very elegant. "Washed gloves" refers to gloves imported from France or Spain where by a special process
they had been impregnated with a permanent perfume. The
trouble and expense required to furnish such articles as

compartmented headdresses, leather-soled buskins and
fancy gloves shows that little was spared in making the
Revels shows detailed productions. That imported, perfumed gloves were used suggests especially what pains
were taken to assure a convincing elegance.

It has been mentioned above (page sixteen) that Revels
costumes were considered suitable for use in social functions. A fact which would also tend to confirm the careful
workmanship expended on them is that they were frequently
stolen. There are several references in the accounts to
players, as well as the amateur performers of the masks,
"carryinge away of costumes." (Documents 1908: 24).

Characterization

The accounts describe various costumes in inventory
form. From these descriptions an excellent idea of the
complete dress of a few stage characters can be obtained.[10]
A Turkish magistrate wore a long straight gown of red
cloth of gold. It was festooned with roses and scallop
shells and striped and edged with broad borders of red
dornixe, which were embroidered with gold cloth and silver thread. The border was edged with black silk lace.
The gown had long sleeves of the same material, red cloth
of gold, which hung low at the wrist. The close-fitting
undersleeves were of gold cloth ornamented with figures
made of white, red and green velvet. A cape, probably in
the form of a short, semi-circular cloak, made of the
same material as that of the undersleeves, gold cloth,
was also worn.

One of Acteon's six assistant hunters wore a pair of
slops (very bulky, loose breeches) and a sleeved jerkin
(a close-fitting jacket) of purple-gold cloth. Both garments were lined with white-gold sarsenet and festooned
with green velvet cut into leave shapes. His buskins were
of orange velvet with copper buttons. He wore a hunting
cloak, undoubtedly contemporary in style, of black-gold
cloth woven with tinsel and fringed with gold silk. His
headpiece had a "top" part of yellow-gold sarsenet

festooned with tufts of yellow and green feathers and fringed with gold. The headpiece was decorated, perhaps encircled, with leaves cut out of green-gold sarsenet. He carried a spear with a shaft made of painted wood and a point made of papier mâché covered with metal foil. It was fringed with silver and silk.

One of eight clowns who performed in a mask wore a crimson satin coat edged with yellow-gold lawn (a fine, costly linen). It had half sleeves of the same lawn material and undersleeves of green damask lined with lawn and turned back at the cuffs. His hose matched the undersleeves. The shoes were of black velvet laced around the ankle. He wore a broad hat of crimson satin lined with green-gold sarsenet to match his coat, as well as an apron, essentially similar in form to one of today, of white-gold sarsenet fringed with gold. He carried either a flail or a spade made of foiled wood. One would not describe as subtle a costume made of crimson, yellow-gold, green, green gold, white and black colors; but the hues are not inharmonious and must have presented an appropriately theatrical effect under the bright candlelight used in the Revels productions.

Torchbearers were also elaborately attired. One torchbearer costume (Documents 1908: 39) consisted of a pair of crimson damask slops lined with white damask and a gown of murrey damask with long pendant sleeves. The sleeves were paned with green satin and revealed undersleeves of crimson to match the slops. The cuffs and hem of the gown were fringed with yellow and green Parisian silk. The clown's headpiece, made of plain white sarsenet and lined with green taffeta, was covered with ivy leaves cut out of green-gold and silver cloth. The importance of different torchbearers was probably indicated by slight variations in their costumes. For, while six out of eight torchbearers — eight was an average number for a mask — wore the costume just described, two of the eight had undersleeves and slops of murrey satin rather than of crimson damask. It is impossible to tell from the accounts whether the torchbearers furnished needed illumination or merely dressed the stage. In each of the masks ther appears to be an equal number of performers and torchbearers. Thus it may be assumed that the staging of a mask was in some ways consistently stylized.

There are other characters cited in the accounts. It is hard to imagine how the Elizabethan audiences recognized the various characters; but if they did recognize them by dress, the means of recognition must have been particular traditionalized symbols associated with each character rather than any historical accuracy of dress as it is known today. A complete list will show the types of costumes required by masks alone. Each costume was probably as elaborate as any of those described above:

| | |
|---|---|
| mariners | Albanese warriors |
| Hungarians | Turkish archers |
| Dianas | Irish kerns |
| nymphs | swart rutters |
| patriarchs | huntresses |
| Germans | Venuses |
| fishermen | palmers |
| Turkish magistrates | Nusquams |
| Venetian senators | sumpners |
| astronomers | Acteons |
| Barbarians | clowns |
| conquerors | graziers |
| Moors | drum-and-fifers |
| Greek worthies | minstrels |
| Venetian commoners | Italian ladies |
| market wives | shipmen |
| country maids | lanceknights |
| foresters | devils |
| sages | Amazons |

There is a statement in the accounts that a costume "never come before her heyghness twysse In on forme." (Documents 1908: 409). This means that many of the old costumes were altered beyond recognition for use in new

24

shows. The accounts list several transformations or
"translations" of costumes. For example, the costumes
of the Turkish magistrates described above were remade
for a Mask of Astronomers and then again remade for a
Mask of Barbarians. The dress of six Greek Worthies
was subsequently transformed into costumes of con-
querors and, later, into Moorish dress. The hanging
sleeves of the Venetian senators, made of tissue gold
figured with silver and decorated with gold and red velvet, were made into headpieces and undersleeves for
Turks, and then into shoes. Similarly, the green-silver
cloth which had been used to make the legs of mariners'
slops was subsequently used for the lining of Germans'
slops, for paning fishermen's suits, for another mariners
mask and, finally, for the torchbearers in a Turkish Mask.
It would take an observant Court to recognize the old materials in such altered forms. The transformations are
evidence that in spite of richness of costume an attempt
was made at economy.

Before the subject of costumes is left, a distinction
should be made between the costumes of masks and those
of plays. The masks, being performed largely by amateurs, had to be completely outfitted by the Revels Office.
The fact that gentlemen and ladies appeared in them meant
that fine gloves and similarly expensive items had to be
supplied. Moreover, costumes were the sine qua non of
the mask genre. On the other hand, the actors of plays,
particularly the noblemen's troups, furnished many of
their own costumes. In 1571-72 all the plays of the season were "throwghly apparelled and ffurnished" (Documents 1908: 409) by the Revels Office. In other years,
such as 1579-80, the Revels clerk seems to have distinguished between plays "wholie furnyshed in this offyce"
and plays furnished with "sondrie" or "many" things
(Chambers 1923: 225). The Master of the Revels chose
most plays for court performance from the repertories
of the professional companies. Although these plays were
often revised by the Master, it would seem unlikely that

25

they were completely recostumed. Indeed, the expense accounts of some plays do not mention costumes at all.

The noblemen's companies did, of course, have their own costumes. And there is no reason to believe that these costumes were in any way inferior to those of the Revels Office. The gentlemen of Gray's Inn rented costumes from the Revels in 1572, as did other groups outside the Court. This practice was annoying to one of the costume manufacturers of London, one Thomas Gylles, who write in protest to the Queen (Documents 1908: 410). One of the main values of the Revels accounts is the light they may shed on the practices of independent companies. Certainly in respect to costume the accounts suggest the use of elaborate costumes by those companies. Many of their costumes and many of the Revel's must have been interchangeable.

## IV. SCENERY

Any attempt to settle the problem of the exact nature of Elizabethan stage scenery becomes immensely complicated. The following discussion will be confined almost entirely to the information presented in the Revels accounts. Some attempt will be made to interpret it, however, in the light of other sources.

Familiarity with the prose of the accounts produces a respect for the specificity of Elizabethan vocabulary. One of the clerks of the Revels, Edward Buggyn, in 1571-72, states about as well as anyone could the general manner of scenic production (Documents 1908: 145):

> All which vi playes . . . being so orderly
> addressed were lykewise throwghly apparelled,
> and ffurnished, with sundry kindes, and sutes
> of apparell, and furniture, fitted and garnished
> necessarely, and answerable to the matter,
> person and parte to be played: having also apt
> howses: made of canvasse, fframed, ffashioned

and paynted accordingly, as mighte best
serve theier severall purposes.  Together
with sundry properties incident, ffashioned,
paynted, garnished, and bestowed as the
partyes them selves required and needed.

As will be shown, other large scenic structures, in addition to the houses, were built.

## Models

It is surprising to learn that the Revels Office used
such apparently modern devices as miniature models, or
maquettes, for its scenery.  There is mention in the accounts of the construction and alteration of a model for a
banquet house; the work required the services over a period of eight days of an artist and his helper (Documents
1908: 93).  They received twentypence and sixteenpence
per day respectively.  Individual pieces of decor were also modeled, for there is listed a sum paid for "models for
a mounte" (Documents 1908:  340).  It is hard to distinguish between the meanings of the terms used:  "model,"
"pattern" and "plotte."  What a model was seems fairly
clear from the fact that wainscot was used to construct
one (Documents 1908:  81).  There are mentioned "patternes and plottes" and "patternes of Chariott and mounte
. . with colors and accessories" (Documents 1908:  157-
160).  The plots were perhaps groundplans and the patterns
probably colored drawings in elevation.  Patterns, however, might also have been tracing forms or stencils, perhaps in classical style.  That "patterns" was actually a
generic term for any type of design is shown in the entry
"patternes . . for strange men, painting them" (Documents
1908: 204).  Most of the production accounts mention a
sum paid for a model or pattern; and several accounts include travel expenses for designers who were required to
travel frequently from the Revels workshops and back
again for the purpose of revising their work.  Whatever
their exact nature, the use of models of all sorts shows

an interest in both economy and artistic planning. By no means every stage designer today makes maquettes for his scenery.

## Houses

The most noteworthy fact that emerges from the statement quoted above is that the stage houses were made of canvas stretched on frames. The frames were made of spars, which were pole-like pieces of timber, rectangular and of moderate thickness. One listing of lumber mentions "elme boordes and 7 ledges for frames" (Documents 1908: 218). Other woods beside elm were probably used for the spars. Poles of fir, by comparison, were used for the rails of a battlement. What the seven "ledges" were is uncertain, but it is tempting to conjecture that they were pieces of molding intended to be attached at the tops of the frames to reproduce cornices. The spars were joined by nails or, as was more likely, by screws called "vices." "Vices for the frames" is a common item in the accounts. Nuts and washers are also mentioned, implying that bolts were used. The wiredrawer, aside from the above mentioned hardware, supplied nails, which were used to "strayne the Canvas" onto the frames (Documents 1908: 201). It is probable that glue, often listed in the accounts, was also used, as it is today, for attaching the canvas permanently to the frames.

It is evident that the houses were not made of the more or less standardized flat frames, called "flats" in modern theater parlance. The accounts would almost certainly have had a more particular name than "frames" for such interchangeable pieces. Also, flats are better adapted to interior walls than to the distinctively different exteriors indicated (as will be seen hereafter) by the accounts as well as by the stage directions of the plays of the time. Furthermore, larger pieces of timber, such as rafters and double quarter-boards were used to make some of the scenery. The latter, commonly used in carpentry as uprights, measured four inches wide by four inches thick.

This size implies heavier and more solidly built units than the easily portable modern flat. Moreover, the houses were three-dimensional and thus made to stand by themselves; flats are made to reproduce two dimensional interior walls.

The accounts indicate, as do the stage directions of plays of the time, that the houses were used for entrances and exits and that the players did not merely parade in front of them. In this respect, the question of the depth of the houses arises. An illuminating entry mentions "a payle [pail] for a castell topp" (Documents 1908: 203). This would indicate that the houses definitely had depth and thus probably three sides. Although "payle" may refer to the Oxford English Dictionary's second meaning: a fence made of stakes, a paling, or a palisade. More importantly, however, the entry indicates that the houses, or castles in this case, were made in reduced scale; that is, in the size of large miniature buildings. Such was the medieval tradition (Nicoll 1931: 196).[11] Reduced buildings were evidently not objectionable: the senate house used for the play Titus and Gesippus, in 1576, contained only two benches for the senators. Evidently, the stage houses, in respect to size, were symbolic.

Feuillerat calculates (Feuillerat 1910: 70) by dividing the number of yards of canvas bought by the number of houses built in a season, that the average house used about sixteen square yards of canvas. He adds that that figure should be reduced since some of the canvas was used in making curtains, mountains and other decor which required disproportionate amounts of cloth. A convenient year for computation, which Feuillerat does not consider, is 1573-74. In February of that year forty ells, or fifty yards, of canvas were bought to make the houses for two plays. If the canvas came in yard widths, as Feuillerat assumes, fifty square yards would be enough to make five houses, each ten feet high, five feet wide, and two and a half feet deep. Such a house would use ten square yards of canvas. If the house were intended to be a castle, a pail-sized turret would conveniently fit its scale.

The houses were painted with gold and silver as well as the more ordinary colors.  Glue, sizing and various colors are common entries in the accounts; and often the pigments are given:  such poetically named hues as verdigris, masticote (a yellow pigment), bice (dark blue), sinoper (red), etc.  The fact that oil never appears as an article used in painting or scenery leads one to believe that dry pigments were mixed with water and glue, as they are in most scene shops today.

The complexity of the painting work itself is indicated by the number of painters employed in the preparation of each season's scenery.  Next to tailors, painters comprise the largest group of workmen hired by the Revels Office.  For the season of 1571-72 an average of fourteen men worked eighteen days and eight nights to paint the scenery for six plays.  (This statement is based on the assumption, explained above, that the masks which followed the plays each night did not require separate scenic houses.)  In 1572-73 eight plays were produced, requiring an average of fourteen painters working seventeen days and six nights.  When we realize that a working day at the Revels Office at the time of Elizabeth was ten hours long, and a working night six, (Documents 1908: 12),[12] our appreciation of the painting work increases.  These figures translated into modern labor conditions would mean that fourteen men worked about four days (of eight hours) to paint the scenery for a single play.  If each play required, say, three houses, each house must have received a good deal of the painters' attention.  It is difficult to learn just what kind of painting work was performed.  Obviously the gilding of moldings, cornices and architraves (see the quotation below) took some pains; but it is likely, if such was the only detailed work required, that a single workman could easily paint a "house" in one day.  The names of the painters hired by the Revels formed at times extensive lists, which, as they are recorded in the accounts, indicate that each painter received fifteenpence per day.

Tailors received twelvepence, carpenters fourteen and propertymakers, embroiderers and haberdashers eighteen. All this suggests that the painters were not original creative artists but that they performed some special time-consuming task. It is likely that their job involved the copying or transferral of patterns or designs created by the scene designer. (See Models, above.) If a special painting or scene was required, an individual artist was probably hired. We find that an artist named Arnolde was paid twenty shillings for "Andramedas picture" (Documents 1908: 181). The picture was painted on a "great cloth" of canvas, which probably served as a backdrop. It is Lily Campbell's opinion (Campbell 1923: chapter 3) that the painters painted classical motifs on the scenery in the manner of Serlio, who recommended the use of patterns. Whatever the precise nature of the designs, it is obvious that the painting was rich and elaborate. The Elizabethan court stage setting was neither haphazard, plain or sketchy but fully planned, ornate and finished.

There is disagreement about the nature of the ornament used on the stage houses. Fortunately, the Revels accounts shed some light on that subject. The following entry is the most precise description of scenery in the accounts (Documents 1908: 158):

> paynting A castell –x s the Rock and Churche
> in the Castle –x s. The pillers Arcatrye
> frize cornish and the Roofe gilt with golde
> and fine silver –c s./ the Armes of England
> and ffraunce upon it –x s/

This surprisingly exact differentiation of architectural details shows a knowledge of the classical orders. The richness of the painting is also indicated, as is the symbolic decoration. It is evident from paintings of late medieval plays that classical architectural details were used on stage (Wickham 1959: plate XXVIII). Certain "ledges" used, perhaps, for making moldings or cornices for the frames have already been discussed.

31

The houses could be fanciful enough to include fringes as part of their decoration. One entry reads "frenge for the players house (Documents 1908: 244).

The variety of types of structures, evidently of a distinct traditional nature in the minds of the Revels workmen, shows that distinctions were made in ornament, and probably decorative painting, as well as in general shape. The following types of buildings are mentioned:

### Large buildings

| | | |
|---|---|---|
| Strato's house | a palace | 3 castles |
| Gobbyn's house | an emperor's palace | a large castle |
| Orestes' house | Prosperity's palace | a castle of Peace |

### Rural scenery

| | | |
|---|---|---|
| 3 country houses | 2 woods | a holly tree |
| forests | a desert | |
| hollow trees | 2 arbors | |

### Groups of houses

| | | |
|---|---|---|
| 15 cities | several towns | a Scotland |
| 3 large cities | the city of Rome | |

### Miscellaneous items

| | | |
|---|---|---|
| a hell | 5 mountains | 2 prisons |
| a hell mouth | a Parnassus | 2 senates |
| a heaven | 3 rocks | |
| heaven with | | |
| clouds | 2 wells | |
| 16 battlements | 4 war tents | |

Two things are evident in the preceding list which tend to confirm what has been said earlier: the houses in their various forms were obviously functional miniatures, since "Scotland" or "the city of Rome" could not be represented full-size on any stage; as such, the houses were carefully painted and ornamented to represent contemporary ideas of traditional edifices.

## Perspective

The question arises whether perspective was attempted in the construction, painting and arrangement of the stage houses. The qualifications of a Master of the Revels, as set forth in one of the organizational charts of the office, are suggestive (Documents 1908: 11):

> The connynge of the office resteth in skill
> of devise, in undertaking of historyes, in
> judgment of comedies, tragedyes and shows,
> in sight of perspective and architecture, some
> smack of geometry and other thinges whereof
> the best helpe is for the officers to make good
> choice of cunynge artificers.

Lily Campbell believes that the above statement plus the Revel's distinction between "town" or "city" and "country house" plus the use of patterns, silk flowers and much cardboard all indicate that Serlio's Architettura was read by the Revels officers. If Serlio's ideas on perspective expressed therein were being followed, the stage houses would have been designed carefully according to scale and painted and placed in a manner to suggest, to at least one central location in the audience, streets in receding perspective. Wings and a backdrop painted to scale would have been required.

An interesting entry for the year 1568 reads, "Scotlande and a great castell one thother side" [of the stage]. This is an important entry, because it indicates that the pieces of stage scenery called houses were placed at separate points on the stage. In other words, a Serlian unity was not achieved. The stage directions of such plays as Endymion and Ralph Roister-Doister corroborate the use of independently placed houses. In a dissertation called The Court and the London Theaters During the Reign of Elizabeth, T. Graves expresses his conviction that the placing of stage houses was traditional and non-perspectival. Furthermore, the use of natural foliage in the court plays, shown by an entry reading, "Cariage of trees

and other things to the Coorte for a Wilderness in A
playe" (Documents 1908:  180), would make difficult the
integration of Serlian perspective.  The system of separated, independent houses placed on stage at the same
time is called simultaneous setting.  Feuillerat is definite
about its use on the Revels stages (Feuillerat 1910:  175):

> Il n'est pas douteux que la décoration
> simultanée était le système adopté pour
> les représentations de la cour.  Le récit
> de Bereblock est très net sur ce point:  "Ex
> utroque scenae latere," a-t-il dit,  "comoedis
> ac personatis magnifica palatia aedesque ap-
> paratissimae extruuntur."

It may be said in summary that, although Serlian perspective might have been used late in Elizabeth's reign,
the normal practice was to place about the stage at suitable places houses differentiated by ornament and painted
designs into palaces, prisons, etc., which houses were
perforce not life-size and built neither in scale with one
another nor to be placed in any overall perspective.  The
effect was essentially an indoor version of the medieval
simultaneous setting.

Scenic Effects

Sometimes the scene designer transformed the stage
into a unique locale.  Most noteworthy in this respect is
the construction of large "mounts" or mountains on the
stage.  The Knight of the Burning Rock, given during the
season of 1578-79, used a rock in which was burned aqua
vitae.  Feuillerat believes (Feuillerat 1910:  71) that the
action took place on the rock, since a seat for "the burning
knight" and an assault ladder are mentioned also.  The
frame for the rock used two posts of quarterboard (two
inches by four inches), four posts of double quarterboard
(four inches by four inches), thirty-two deal boards
(three inches by eight inches by six feet), a hundred fifty-
three of elm board and several disks of elm (Documents
1908:  306-310 passim).  Hoops also were often used for

such constructions. An even greater structure must have been built in 1572, when a rock contained a well and Apollo and the nine muses (Documents 1908: 157). Two thousand one hundred twenty-five nails of different sizes were used to assemble the boards, which, once dismantled, filled two commercial transport wagons. A mountain was used in 1581 which supported a dragon with artificial fire, a château with collapsible sides, a tree with shields, a hermitage, a hermit, savages and a magician (Documents 1908: 345-346). Forests were sometimes reproduced on stage. There is mention of artificial boughs, flowers made of silk and of artificial hollow trees from which performers would emerge (Documents 1908: 197, 200, 203). Real foliage was also used, as indicated above; also found is "a tree of Holly" and "holly for a forest" (Documents 1908: 175). Ivy, moss, and oak boughs were also used. Whether the whole stage was thus transformed into a forest is not certain; but such an enterprise was certainly not beyond the imagination of the Revels officers. The decoration of a banquet house built for Montmorency's visit in 1572 shows that a great deal of foliage was used indoors. All sorts of flowers, leaves and boughs were gathered and attached to the wainscotted walls of the banquet house. Even greenery imported from Scotland was used. The stage designers would certainly not hesitate to transform whole scenic areas into woods, if such would "most lyvely expresse the effect of the histories played. "

The ingeniousness of the burning rock has already been mentioned, as has the château with collapsible sides and the hollow trees. The stage directions of W. Percy's Faery Pastorall, performed in 1603, give a good idea of how the hollow tree worked (Feuillerat 1910: 79):

Hippolon Running in on winding of Hornes
from severall places of the Forest shoued
off with his shoulder the Pin wherewith the
oake was shute, then fell down himself
wearied to Death. and Picus came furth
the oake.

35

One of the rocks used in the Revels shows was provided with a fountain. That the fountain ran with water is indicated by the entries "for a pipe for water" and "cast pipes and soder" (Documents 1908: 368-369). This kind of scenery, as well as the traditional hell mouth and its flames, suggest the element of pleasing surprise that must have accompanied some of the special effects. Thunder and lightning were also produced. One artisan was paid for "his device in counterfeiting Thunder and Lightning in the plays of Narcisses . . " (Documents 1908: 142). Also somewhat surprising must have been the entrance of the pageant cars and the sudden revealing of their occupants, an effect sometimes produced by the dropping of a curtain suspended from the roof of the car.

The larger pageant cars, particularly those with curtains, would have constituted virtually a momentary change of scene. They would probably be conceived of in modern theater vernacular as "mobile insets." The stage houses themselves could be mobile, as in the case of "A castell for Lady peace to sytt and be browghte in before the Queenes Maiestie" (Documents 1908: 202). A similar means of changing the scene, and in this case to an interior, is seen in the use of "senate houses." The senate constructed for the play Titus and Gesippus contained two benches for the senators. The senates were often constructed with a curtain, which could be drawn back to reveal the occupants inside (Documents 1908: 140, 276, 296). (The accounts list "curtyn ringes" and "lynes to draw curtains with" (Documents 1908: 140, 202).) In the above ways a kind of scenic flow or pace could be maintained, much the same as that furnished by the use of insets in the modern theater.

One of the most complicated and ambitious machines, however, appears to have been the cloud used in the season of 1578-79. The cloud was borrowed by the Revels Office and altered to fit either the court stage frame or the rock onto which it could have been lowered. There is mention of "linnen blue and hoops to mend cloud"

(Documents 1908: 308). That the cloud did actually rise and descend is shown by the reference "pulleys and drawing up and down a cloud" (Documents 1908: 307). Baskets, perhaps disguised as clouds, were also suspended: the entries read "a rope, a pulley, a basket" (Documents 1908: 146) and "Baskett with 4 Eares handles to hang Dylligence in" (Documents 1908: 199). Thus it is possible the cloud also supported the weight of a person representing some allegorical virtue. The cloud required long boards made into a "steer," undoubtedly a device meant to guide the cloud in its descent or in its lateral progress across the stage. A sun was used during the same season and may have been similarly suspended. The use of descending clouds reveals the important fact that the court stages were constructed with a superstructure sturdy enough to fly some kinds of scenic devices.

It is difficult to determine the use to which the oft mentioned curtains were put. It is clear that they were worked by cord and pulleys and used to disclose the occupants of pageant wagons and such insets as senate houses. The curtains were fringed, as might be expected (Documents 1908: 200). Plays such as Sapho and Phao show that curtains were used to conceal the occupants of an alcove, probably placed at the back of the stage. Sapho, extended on her bed says to her attendants that she wants to sleep: "Draw the curtain," she cries (Rothwell 1953: 178-181). Were front curtains used? William Rothwell asserts (Rothwell 1953: 178-181) that front or proscenium-type curtains were sometimes used in Renaissance plays and that the custom was to open them or to let them fall at the beginning of a play, in which state they remained until the end of the last act. There is perhaps some evidence for a similar usage by the Revels Office. There is mention of "one greate curteyne, one mountaine, one greate cloth of canvass" (Documents 1908: 365). This suggests that the mountain, probably occupying the major part of the stage, was revealed by a "greate curteyne" hung in front of it. The "great cloth of canvass" was

37

perhaps a painted backdrop, like the one of "Andramadas picture." One curtain was made of eight ells of double sarsenet (Documents 1908: 336), which would be enough material to furnish conveniently a piece of cloth twelve feet high by fifteen feet long. This seems about right for an alcove, but perhaps was sufficient also for a front curtain. It is certainly possible that a superstructure used to fly clouds and people was also used for the hanging of a "great" front curtain.

Little or nothing is given in the Revels accounts which indicates the nature of the stage proper. It must have had a superstructure, as just indicated, and must have been wide and deep enough to hold the various houses, mounts, prisons, arbors, etc. mentioned above. It must have been elevated to provide for the trap-door effects called for in plays of the time. Since the Office of Works handled the actual building of the stage, the Revels accounts are not helpful. The Works accounts themselves are incomplete; one entry, however, is useful (Feuillerat 1910: 74):

> newe making and setting up of Scaffoldes,
> particians, and dores and other necessaries
> for the Maundayes, Playes, Tragedyes,
> Maskes, Revelles and Tryumphes at divers
> and sondry tymes.

If a simultaneous setting is assumed, the partitions may have been the large back and side walls of the stage frame in front of which were set the houses and other decor. The door would then have been such as to admit the actors to the general acting area in front of and between the houses. The stages were placed at one end of the great halls of various royal palaces. (See Section I above.) The average dimensions of the halls used were forty by one hundred five feet. Thus wide stages might have been used. The "Entertainment at Cambridge" (Nichols 1788: I, 166) discloses that the whole width of the chapel of King's College was used for a play, so that the side chapels served as "houses." Conjectures about the specific nature of the stage can be lengthy; to continue the present discussion, however, would detract from the information given in the Revels accounts, which, in effect, say little about the stage itself.

A summary of the foregoing information about scenery should include the following points. A raised stage with a sturdy superstructure was used. It might have been as wide as forty feet and might have included a front curtain. An alcove might have been placed at the rear. Various kinds of insets, some curtained, were used: such as senate houses, pageant cars and prisons. Mobile houses were also used. Large and elaborate rocks, mountains, forests as well as particular special scenic effects were also exploited. Most plays would require two or three scenic houses placed on opposite sides of the playing area and, probably, along the rear extremity of it, or "upstage." The houses were three-dimensional and large enough for the players to use, but in effect miniature units as compared with real buildings. They were in neither scale nor perspective, and many were both medieval and classical in detail. They were made of intricately and richly painted canvas stretched on wooden frames. They would vary in design to indicate all kinds of buildings and building groups from Rome to a battlement or country house. The whole setting would be simultaneous rather than successive, and so would differ basically from the effect produced by most modern realistic settings.

## V. PROPERTIES

In the accounts the makers of properties are grouped under the heading "propertymakers, inbroders and haberdashers;" but it is convenient to distinguish what, in effect, constituted the third logical task of the Revels – the fabrication of articles, not of clothing, carried on and off stage by the performers or used by them on the stage. In modern theater parlance a distinction is made between hand and stage properties, which serves generally to distinguish between lighter articles, such as a sword, and heavier objects, such as a well. Sometimes it is difficult to distinguish a stage property from a piece of scenery; the former, however, is usually operated in some way by an actor. As usual it is impossible to tell from the accounts just what properties were used in a given mask or play. Furthermore, all the articles used are probably not accounted for, since articles already on hand would not be mentioned in the accounts. It is reasonable to suppose that properties were reused; although, if the same concern for novelty which caused the continual alteration of costumes operated in the case of properties, the old properties were altered beyond recognition. Some of the more cumbersome items were probably more expensive to store than to dismantle. As in the case of modern theaters, the Revels office probably found it efficient to keep some of the more common items.

Whatever articles were preserved, the property storeroom of the Revels must have been well stocked. Feuillerat believes (Feuillerat 1910: 61) that it would rival the most encumbered property room of the most renowned modern theater. A good idea of the variety and extent of the properties can be had from a list of various articles used during the years from 1558 to 1589. The list is not complete, but includes most of the items mentioned in the accounts:[13]

Either hand or stage properties

| 1. Human forms | 2. Animal forms | |
|---|---|---|
| devils eyes | stuffed fishes | unicorn's horn |
| head of Mercury | thornbacks | wings of ostrich |
| heads | flounders | feathers |
| iced heads[14] | mackerels | a dragon |
| bodies of men in | dragon head | an artificial |
| timber | beasts | lion |
| wax figures | serpents | horse of wood |
| stuffed canvas | hound's head | hobby horses |
| form | lion's head | monsters |

40

# REVELS ACCOUNTS

## Stage properties

| | | |
|---|---|---|
| desk | tree of silk | chariots |
| table | well | clouds |
| altar | basket with | sun |
| rocks | handles | heaven |
| gibbet | fountain | scaling ladder |
| arbor | great hollow | hanging lock |
| hell mouth | trees | and key |
| tree of holly | wheat sheaves | |

## Hand properties

**1. Weapons**
swords
darts
daggers
bows
arrows
falchions
bills
shields
scabbards
mace
knives
halberds
borespears
pollaxes
clubs
rapiers
javelins
axes
guns

**2. Poles, etc.**
crogerstaves
scepters
bannerstayes
marshalls'
   staves
palmers' staffs
wands
poles
a truncheon
hunters' staffs

**3. Musical
   instruments**
horns
trumpets
gilt bugles
drum
cornet
silver whistle

**4. Allegorical**
stick bundle
key
olive branch
crystal
   shield
crowns
mirrors
scythe
bolt, shackle,
   collar
gold chains

**5. Miscellaneous**

hand balls
targets
banners
ensigns
spurrs
gloves
nets
rings
pitchers
platters
trays
baskets

41

                                                    flasks
                                                    bottles
                                                    false foods
                                                    fruit, eggs,
                                                        cake, etc.
                                                    feather-flowers
                                                    chimney-
                                                        sweeper
                                                    brushes

   A number of things are obvious in the above lists.
First of all, there is a special interest in the imitation or
representation of men and animals.  Although live animals
probably were also used, the number of false heads and
bodies shows that there were special uses.  One use might
have been the dismemberment or mutilation of bodies, an
act required often in the enactment of brutalities and battle
scenes.  Another use was surely allegorical:  stationary
human and animal forms representing various abstract
forces which could not well be imitated by real animals.
Secondly, the number of different weapons shows the ex-
actness with which combats were represented.  One of the
official duties of the Revels Office was the outfitting of
tournaments.  Many of the weapons listed above were
probably used in a triumph or tournament; but there is
little reason to doubt that the purely dramatic combats, if
less dangerous, were any less authentic.  One of the most
common property entries is swords of various kinds: evidently a large element of theatrical interest was military
show.  Thirdly, the elaborate and distinct qualities of
some of the articles is quite evident.  In a Mask of Fishermen[15] the propertymakers distinguished between thorn-
backs, flounders and mackerels; the counterfeit eggs and
cake must also have looked quite real; similarly, the different musical instruments are differentiated.[16]  Finally,
there appears in the accounts a kind of allegorical apparatus of properties.  In a modern property room one would
find such useful items as a telephone, a mantlepiece,
suitcases, etc.  In the Revels accounts one finds the

equally essential olive branches, hell's mouth, scythe, etc.
These items made up part of the standard scenic vocabulary
of Renaissance times and as such were probably preserved
from show to show.

A great deal of importance was attached to the emble-
matic decoration of tournaments. Chambers remarks
(Chambers 1923: I, 148) that the "accession tilt of 1613 is
made memorable by the fact that the Earl of Rutland had
the signal honour of being furnished with an impresa by
the united genius of Shakespeare and Burbage, whom we
must presume to have been the poet and the painter respectively." Chambers remark is based on the Rutland
MSS iv, 494, which reads:

> Item 31 Martii to Mr. Shakespeare in gold
> about my Lords impresso xliiijs. To Richard
> Burbage for paynting and making it in gold
> xliiijs.

Some of the larger stage properties show how ambitious court productions could be. In addition to what has
been said above under the section on Scenery, it is well
to mention the hell mouth, a traditional medieval stage
piece. One hell mouth mentioned in the accounts contained
"fierworks" (Documents 1908: 140), which was probably
created by the burning of aqua vitae, as in the case of the
burning rock, mentioned above. (See Scenery.) If the
mouth resembled those shown in medieval paintings, it
was a fiercely toothed, fish-like aperture which opened
about as wide as a man's height. Also worthy of mention
are the monsters, which were made of hoops and canvas
and were sometimes mobile. There is the record of the
sum of two shillings sixpence paid to one Benbow for
"playing in the monster" (Documents 1908: 176). There
is also mention of a "dragon with fierworks" (Documents
1908: 345).

A common stage piece, mentioned above in the discussion on scenery, was the traditional chariot or pageant.
These were large decorated wagons, somewhat resembling

modern parade floats, which were wheeled or drawn onto
the stage or among the audience.  The use of a typical
chariot can be seen in one of the descriptions in the Revels
accounts (Documents 1908:  157):

> Chariott of xiiii foote Long and viii foote
> brode with a Rock upon it and a fountayne
> therein with the furnishing and garnishing
> thereof for Apollo and the Nine Muses.

The base of a chariot such as this was probably rectangular
and rather near the floor (Wickham 1959:  plate XIX).  On
it were placed the fountain and mountain in which were hol-
lowed seats for the muses.  Over all there was likely to be
a rectangular canopy supported at each corner by a pillar
rising from the base.  On the page following the above
quotation there is record of a sum paid "for gilding iiii
pillers of a waggon."  If the pillars were themselves gilded,
the rest of the car must have been equally rich and elaborate.  Pictures of pageants of the time (Wickham 1959:
plate XIX) show elaborately carved classical moldings
and ornaments.  The pageant cars must have contained
curtains, for there is record of a "Rocke, or hill for the
ix muses to Singe uppone" and a curtain or "Vayne of
Sarsnett Drauuen upp and downe before them" (Documents
1908:  277).  Similar to the cars, though probably stationary, was an "Harbour for Lords (Documents 1908:  117),
probably a formalized, symmetrical unit of artificial or
real foliage.

Other stage properties such as the well and gibbet are
typical of the kind of devices used in the Renaissance productions of plays and masks.  Similar items must have
been inherited from earlier days of court entertainment
and so were not listed in the accounts.  Since most of the
scenes were exteriors, little ordinary furniture was used.
Feuillerat believes (Feuillerat 1910:  64) that furniture and
weapons used in the Revels shows were usually rented or
bought.  A well was definitely rented from an inn called
"the Bell in gracious streets" (Documents 1908:  277).

It has been mentioned above that a cloud was also borrowed. Numerous tricks were used by the Revels artificers to counterfeit real objects. Gold and silver foil was used to make objects look like metal. Swords were often made from wainscot and then covered with foil (Documents 1908: 261). Armor was also counterfeited. Silver money was produced by foiling paper disks (Documents 1908: 246). Snowflakes were simulated by thin-pressed sugar and hail stones by lumps of sugar (Documents 1908: 175). Balls of snow were made of bombast covered with lambskin. Sometimes they contained sponges perfumed with rose water (Documents 1908: 175-178). Flowers and leaves were frequently made of silk. In general, then, the Revels workmen showed as much, if not more, ingenuity in making their properties as any workmen today. They also used the same materials as today: the accounts mention cardboard, paste, glue, felt, wax, clay, papier mâché, and, of course gilt and colors.

## VI.  LIGHTING

The Revels plays and masks were, of course, lighted by candles. The chandler received two shillings sixpence for a dozen candles, which weighed three and two tenths ounces each. Today, a cheap candle of that weight is about nine inches long and might burn two hours if free from drafts. This would indicate that the candles were replaced during the course of a theatrical evening, since the entertainment lasted from ten to one and sometimes two in the morning. The large size candelabrum used by the Revels was composed of twenty-four branches, each supporting four lights (Documents 1908: 117). This would be a total of ninety-six candles, a number suggesting that the lights were so small as to require replacement during a three-hour period.

At the base of each candle a round plate was placed, as one is today sometimes, to catch the dripping wax.

There are mentioned "plates" and "double plates," the latter costing tenpence a piece. If ninety-six candles were the usual number used per candelabrum, it would seem from the following entry that as many plates were required:

> Rounde duble plates for the branches that
> hung in the hall and bare lightes, viii doz
> at x v the peece

The plates were sometimes painted, at fourpence the piece (Documents 1908: 140, 276, 296), as well as "turnde in with a crest" (Documents 1908: 140). An interesting item called a "hatte" is mentioned often in the accounts; three entries are instructive: "Plates for walls and for hattes," "ffunnels for hattes with long pypes" and "plates with holes for hattes" (Documents 1908: 202). These entries suggest that a special type of plate was used when a candle was placed near a wall. It was perhaps placed on the wall as is the flat plate or disk of a sconce. "Hats" in modern theater lighting are metal contraptions in the form of a top-hat with the top out; the purpose is to shield and limit the rays of a spotlight. In Elizabethan times, a hat for a candle must have been similar in form but with a part of the side of the crown, rather than the top, missing. Thus it would have been a cyl-inder with a hole in the side. Prongs on the bottom of the hat probably fitted into the holes in the plates, while the "funnels" with "long pipes" (no doubt nar-row flues or spouts) were placed on top of the hats to shield the light above. The whole device might have resem-bled the adjacent drawing:

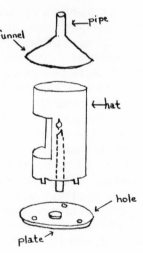

Such devices evidently resembled lanterns, which are mentioned in the accounts. A medium-size one cost three and a half shillings, a large one five shillings (Documents 1908: 276). The significant thing about hatted candles and lanterns is that they must have been used to direct light in a particular direction. Hats, of course, could not be used for each individual candle on a candelabrum, because the illumination coming from the candles behind it would be impeded. Separate candles or several candles placed on one hatted plate might have been used for some effects, although a constantly burning candelabrum overhead would make impossible any dramatic spotlight-like effect. Moreover, only a few hats were used.

The branched candelabra were hung on wires stretched across the hall and tightened by winches and pulleys (Documents 1908: 307-308). How many wires and candelabra were used or just where they were hung in the hall cannot be determined from the Revels accounts. If it is assumed that the great halls already had non-theatrical illumination, then the additional lighting for plays was probably procured by lights hung near or over the stage.

Aside from special hatted candles, lanterns and the usual suspended candelabra, hand torches were used to light the stage. Links, a common item, were torches made of tow (coarse flax yarn) and pitch. It is probable that these were carried by torchbearers. That some torches were placed on candlesticks is shown by the fact that the number of candlesticks ordered for a mask often equals the number of torchbearers, i.e., eight. The accounts mention candlesticks as small, high, vice, stock, prick and hand. The small cost twopence each, the high sixpence, and the vice a shilling. One entry is for four dozen small candlesticks, a number which suggests that the small size was freely used. The effect produced by a masker or player accompanied by two torchbearers can be partially appreciated by a comparison with certain Anglican Church services of today in which the reader of the Epistle is flanked by two candlebearing acolytes.

In church services of Elizabeth's time, and perhaps also in the masks, such illumination was undoubtedly functional. No mention is made in the accounts of either footlights, mirrors or reflectors. If mirrors, in particular, were used to any extent, the accounts would surely have included them. It is possible that the hatted candles and lanterns were used as footlights, a function for which they would appear well adapted, although not sufficiently numerous.

The total effect of the different means of illumination was, according to Feuillerat, "un éclairage éclatant, rivalisant avec la lumière du jour" (Feuillerat 1910: 78). Although the illumination was bright, it is important to keep in mind its quality. Unlike the intense spotlights of today's theater, which can give objects and colors an intense, outstanding brilliance, candles would have produced a softer general illumination. More important, the light could not be well dimmed, increased, directed or otherwise much controlled. This meant that neither expressive changes in the intensity and color of light nor striking contrasts of light and shadow, which modern scenic lighting so much exploits, were possible. Thus the rich detail of the costumes and the intricately decorated scenery were of great importance. The general effect of the lighting must have been more romantic and atmospheric than the harsh effects sometimes employed today.

## VII. THE COURTLY AUDIENCE

Queen Elizabeth's court has been described as "at once gay, decent, and superb" (Hotson 1954: 13). The court consisted of the higher officials of government and their wives, officers of the royal household and their wives, suitors of the Queen, resident foreign ambassadors, ambassadors extraordinary, bachelor courtiers, ladies and maids of honor and other attendants and guests such as the Queen might desire. Most of the court officials and attendants were appointed from among the highest

nobility of England. Since advancement at court, the only
source of high governmental positions, was based on a
highly personal evaluation and preference by the Queen
herself, the serious courtier was expected to spare little
in impressing upon her his intellectual and physical abili-
ties, his education, his personality, his taste and his looks.
 The particularly opulent court held on the night of
January 6, 1600, and the theatrical entertainment given
for it are imaginatively described by Leslie Hotson (Hotson 1954: 65-92). The Italian ambassador from Tuscany,
Don Virginio Orsino, Duke of Bracciano, was present, as
were the Muscovite ambassador from Czar Boris Godunov,
the son of Count Palatine, and the brothers Rohan, heirs
to the Kingdom of Navarre upon the death without issue of
Henry IV of France and his sister. At least twenty-two
English lords were in attendance, including the Arch-
bishop of Canterbury, the Lord Treasurer, Lord Derby,
Lord Worcester and Lord Cumberland. At least twelve
countesses were present, including the countesses of Oxford, Hertford, and Derby. Many other equally and less
exalted of the nobility were also present, as were the
Maids of Honor – young girls of high birth who waited upon
the Queen, talked and read with her, and entertained her
with dancing. The court assembled in the great hall after
supper to watch, according to Hotson, a performance of
Twelfth Night. The hall was richly hung with tapestries
and its walls were lined with the usual tiers of seats. A
musicians' loft was placed on the side wall opposite the
main door of the hall. Hundreds of candles, mostly hung
in branches from the ceiling, illuminated the room.
Elizabeth sat on her dias with Duke Orsino and conversed
with him in Italian, a language in which she was skilled.
In speaking with Elizabeth and his English attendants, the
Muscovite ambassador undoubtedly used Latin. By royal
decree, all the members of the English court were
dressed in white.
 Although the foregoing description, most of which
Hotson bases on documents of the time, is of an unusually

important occasion, it does reveal that Elizabeth's court was composed essentially of powerful people with international manners and fine educations. The linguistic capabilities of Elizabeth herself – including French, Italian and Latin – were reflected among her courtiers, whose knowledge of classical and continental literary and theatrical traditions was unquestionably sophisticated. When these nobles, used to a great deal of pageantry in their daily lives, were dressed in the most ornate of Renaissance costume and assembled on their tiers in a great hall which was itself lavishly appointed, the masks and plays performed for their amusement, even if they did no more than equal the effect of their audience, must have been magnificently imaginative.

## VIII. SUMMARY

The staging of the plays and masks organized by the Revels Office for Queen Elizabeth would have seemed a bit quaint to the modern audience. There was neither scale nor historical consistency in the stage houses; the costumes were equally anachronistic and fanciful; the lighting was overall and undoubtedly yellowish; the music would seem strange to many; and in general the classical and the medieval styles would seem quite confounded. This all comes down to a lack of something taken for granted in modern theater – realism. But it is important to stress that the total effect, though it might seem quaint, would not seem contrived, expressionistic or recherché. In other words, the effect of self-conscious stylization, which figures so strongly in many modern "expressive" productions, would be lacking. To the Elizabethan scene designer the possibilities of invention were not limited to more or less mannered departures from the realistic norm but were increased by the variety of unrestrictive architectural and sartorial motifs. The decor thus attained a unity of its own: neither completely unrelatable make-believe nor completely predictable familiarity (realism)

but the agreeable unity of a reasonably familiar but delight-
fully free splendor.  Thus the plays, which are themselves
inventive and "poetic," to say the least, were in a way reflected in the unselfconscious yet imaginative staging.  The
Revels accounts furnish abundant evidence of the extensive,
elaborate and ingenious nature of such staging at Court.

## NOTES

1.   The inaccuracy of Collier and Cunningham is discussed
at greater length by Feuillerat, as follows:  ". . they [the
Documents] cover the most important period in the history
of the Court drama, and most of them have been published
by Cunningham, or used by Collier.  Both of these editors
are discredited, though constantly, if reluctantly, quoted
for want of more reliable sources.  It was most urgent,
therefore, that somebody should dispel the mist of suspicion
which has for long paralyzed the efforts of many scholars,
when it has not led them into dangerous pitfalls."  In a footnote, Feuillerat adds, 'I am glad to say that in the part of
Cunningham's Revels included in this volume (I leave the
1605 and 1612 Books out of question at present) I have
found no forgery; on the contrary, it is but just to say that
his publication is most accurate, and that I have counted no
more than five or six misreadings.  Unfortunately, I cannot say the same of Collier, as my notes will show."
(Documents 1908:  xi)

2.   The Revels accounts are conveniently divided by Feuillerat into seasons, e.g., 1572-73.  The number of workmen
is artificial, being derived from the total work hours divided by the average number of men working each day.  Page
12 of the Documents states the hours of a work-day and night.

3.   The wages of the officers and workmen are given in any
of the seasonal sections of the Documents.

4.   It is difficult to compare Elizabethan prices with those
of today, because earlier standards of living assigned

different values to many items. Within the Elizabethan framework, however, the relative value of goods and services can be seen.

5. Banquet houses were large tent-like constructions made on occasion of plastered lath walls covered with a canvas roof supported by poles. They were erected by the Revels Office on the palace grounds.

6. He took charge of the two offices from 1509 to 1534, according to Feuillerat.

7. This amount refers to a court or street rather than a stage costume.

8. Almost any listing in the accounts of money paid for cloth will give the price.

9. The Master sometimes rented out Revels costumes for such occasions.

10. Descriptions of this and the following characters are derived from an inventory of costumes on pages 38 to 46 of the Documents.

11. The plate shows stage houses as usable but by no means full size.

12. See note 1 on page 51.

13. The names of the properties are those given in the accounts. The spellings have been modernized, but no attempt to distinguish between overlapping meanings of the terms has been made.

14. Sidney's Arcadia is relevant: "Against whom was the fine frosen Knight, frosen is despaire; but his armor so naturally representing Ice, and all his furniture so lively answering therto, as yet did I never see any thing that pleased me better."

15. Given between 1555 and 1560.

16. The instruments were no doubt used in the Mask of Musicians given between 1555 and 1560.

# RECONSTRUCTIONS OF
# ELIZABETHAN PUBLIC PLAYHOUSES

by

James Stinson

# RECONSTRUCTIONS OF
## ELIZABETHAN PUBLIC PLAYHOUSES

A few years ago Alice Griffin witnessed a performance
of Henry IV, Part One played on the "Elizabethan stage" at
Hofstra College.  Reviewing the production she remarked:

> As the performance gets under way, one
> realizes that whereas our modern staging is
> predominantly horizontal in its visual effects,
> with the action moving from side to side,
> Elizabethan staging made constant use of the
> vertical plane, with movement from the upper
> stages to the platform below.  Thus in tableaux,
> where many or all of the acting areas on the
> vertical plane are used, the effect is similar
> to that of a tapestry or a stained glass window,
> which were familiar Elizabethan media for the
> pictorial representation of important events.
> (Griffin 1956: 139).

Miss Griffin's comment displays her customary acute-
ness, but she is incorrect in assuming that what she saw
was anything more than Hofstra College's idea of Elizabethan staging.  The stage used for that performance was
a five-sixths scale version of the reconstruction of John
Cranford Adams, Hofstra's president.  Although it is still
the best known, Dr. Adams' reconstruction has been chal-
lenged by many other scholars on a number of its funda-
mental assumptions, among the most important of which
is the very principle Miss Griffin singles out for praise.
According to Adams, various acting areas in "the vertical
plane" (as distinct from the platform) were used for as
much as half of many Elizabethan plays.  This notion has
been fairly thoroughly discredited, as we shall see below.
Miss Griffin is correct in saying, "The use of an Elizabethan stage makes it possible to present Shakespearean
plays in the manner of their original presentation," (ibid.
139), but what was that stage like?  We cannot begin to

remotely approximate Elizabethan presentation (assuming that this is desirable) until we know the locations, features, and functions of its various components. The present essay surveys more than two dozen attempts to reconstruct this stage and the theatre of which it was integral part. One conclusion, at least, will be obvious: despite the enormous amount of scholarly energy expended in research on the Elizabethan public playhouse, our present information is so scanty, so vague, and so contradictory that anyone who attempts its reconstruction must be praised for his courage, whatever his conclusions.

In this investigation we must ignore, except in passing, two important areas of activity: full-size theatres and investigations that have not themselves led to reconstructions. This paper does not describe the theatres at the Folger Library and in Ohio, Oregon, California and elsewhere because to do so requires visiting them, and in most cases this has been impossible. Similarly, there is no space to chronicle the vitally important work of men such as W. J. Lawrence, G. F. Reynolds and many others. Reconstructions would be impossible without their work, but they lie beyond our present scope.[1] We are here evaluating a group of attempts to reassemble whole playhouses from the pitiful remains they have left, because it is to these attempts that the student of Renaissance drama usually turns for his picture of Shakespeare's stage.

Before beginning, however, it might be helpful to summarize the various bodies of evidence that are most often drawn upon. Since these groups have never been properly evaluated generically, (and again, we lack the space to do so here) we can only list them and then leave the reader to deal with them as best he can.

First, a number of contemporary maps and views of London proffer tantalizing pictures of some playhouse exteriors. Wretched as they are, they can sometimes tell us something about the size, shape and location of various playhouses. But every one of them is a demonstrably inaccurate drawing, made at a date that must be calculated,

by an artist whose biography and talent are mostly unknown.[2]
The two views most often cited as evidence for one feature
or another of Elizabethan playhouses are the panoramas of
London made by J. C. Visscher and Wenceslaus Hollar in
1616 and 1647, respectively. Both views were engraved
after the burning of the First Globe, and both were printed
on the Continent. The Hollar panorama is by far the more
convincing, but its lateness (the sketches for it were made
around 1644) renders it suspect.

No more satisfactory are the four known sketches of
theatre interiors. In or around 1596, a Dutch traveler,
Johannes de Witt visited the Swan theatre. Because of the
playhouse's similarity to a Roman amphitheatre, he sketched
it and appended a description. Upon De Witt's return to
Utrecht, his friend Arend van Buchell copied the sketch
and description into his own commonplace book. Though
the originals have disappeared, Van Buchell's copies have
survived. It is impossible to tell how faithfully he copied
De Witt's sketch, let along how accurate the lost original
was. The three other drawings are vignettes from the
title pages of plays printed well into the seventeenth century. Two of them, postage stamp-size sketches from
William Alabaster's Latin play Roxanna, 1632, and Na-
thanial Richard's Messalina, 1640, show wedge-shape
stages backed by draw curtains. The artists and the
theatres depicted are unknown. The title page drawing
from The Wits, or Sport upon Sport was made long after
the revolution had closed the playhouses, and is connected
with the Red Bull theatre only by the fact that some of the
play fragments in this collection may have been performed
there surreptitiously, during the Commonwealth. None of
these drawings is verifiably accurate, but still they are
precious documents.[3]

Recently there has been a greatly increased use of
pictorial documentation from related sources: English
masques, pageants and architecture, continental theatres,
processions and tableaux, and medieval drama. The introduction of this material has done much to break down

the insularity of many Shakespearian scholars, but in the same breath it has made the literary investigator responsible for art and theatre history. Too often he has not proved particularly competent in either.

In the area of written records, evidence is still being grubbed up from letters, contracts, lawsuits, pamphlets, diaries and what-not. But here, as with pictorial evidence, the value of these materials is substantially diminished by constant, disheartening ambiguity. For example, in at least two cases, as we shall see below, scholars have differed sharply over the translation of crucial passages in the descriptions of playhouses written by foreigners travelling in England.

The builders' contracts for the Fortune and Hope theatres have survived. The former tells us some basic dimensions of the Fortune's building, stage and galleries, along with incidental information of various kinds. Since the builder, Peter Streete, was also the builder of the recently erected Globe, the contract specifies that a great many of the Fortune's appointments were to be like those at the Globe, and so does not detail them. The contract further infuriates the investigator by referring to an attached "plot" [plan], which of course, has been lost. The Hope contract is shorter and, if possible, even more cryptic.

A favorite hunting preserve for scholars has been the corpus of the drama itself, both text and stage directions. But these sources too, are not without their dangers. In the matter of stage directions, no one is quite sure how they made their way into the texts. One school of opinion, which by now may perhaps be taken to represent orthodox belief, holds that since the compositor in the Elizabethan printing shop set just what he saw in the MS presented to him, directions printed in the margins of plays differ significantly from those interspersed between lines of text. Directions in a text, it is thought, are the playwright's. Notes in the margins, on the other hand, are the insertions of a prompter or book holder, who added them during rehearsals. Apparent support for this notion comes from the theory that the author's directions tend to be imaginative and unspecific while rehearsal directions are laconically practical. Of course, it is the rehearsal directions that are most valuable to the reconstructor, because they constitute actual "blocking" and hence tell us more about stage conditions than the poet's suggestions. The trouble is that this theory is often contradicted by the material it is supposed to explain. It is usually impossible to tell from its nature, who wrote any one direction, and when a guess is possible it often happens that a marginal command is more vaguely expansive than its fellows between the lines of text. Fairly recent work with manuscripts rather than printed texts promises to help clarify the matter, but until it does, we have no adequate method for evaluating stage directions.

The greatest problem with the text itself (aside from its frequent corruptness) is this: how literally are we to take what we find? When A tells B to come down, and B is described as entering, are we to assume that he has descended from some "upper stage" on which he has been visible, or has he simply been out of sight back stage? Too often has one investigator or another thought the text literal where it indicated a feature of his reconstruction and figurative where it contradicted his theory.

Since the evidence in every category is so insubstantial one might suspect that reconstructions should not be attempted at all. Some scholars, notably A.M. Nagler, maintain that any detailed reconstruction must be so misleading as to be worse than worthless (Nagler 1958: 18). These men – constituting the whole body of investigators excluded from present consideration – content themselves with trying to establish the locations, forms and functions of individual parts of the Elizabethan public playhouse. By working this way they escape having to supply every detail, for they know that many major components and almost all less important details must remain the purest conjecture.

Of course, "Elizabethan public playhouses" is no

more than a convenient term for a group of theatres, some
of which were not Elizabethan (the latest we shall consider
were built in 1614) and all of which differed one from
another as theatres inevitably do.[4] Not all of them have
been reconstructed because for some of them little or no
information survives. No one, to my knowledge, has ever
attempted to take a likeness of the first Bear Garden,
Newington Butts, the Rose, or the Red Bull, but reconstructions have been made of the Theatre, the Curtain,
the Swan, the First Globe, the Fortune, the Second Globe,
and the Hope. After surveying the reconstructions of these
theatres we must return to the Elizabethan theatre, because
a number of writers have weighed and sifted the information about all the playhouses and used it to construct "typical" theatres. Of course, since much of the evidence is
contradictory, many of them have availed themselves of
the privilege of using or discarding whatever has suited
their fancies. Actually, reconstructions of the First
Globe fall into this synthetic category, since there is no
reasonably reliable evidence for any of its features. But
the urge to rebuild the playhouse in which sang the sweet
Swan of Avon has been so strong that there have been more
reconstructed "Globe" playhouses than any other theatre.
These attempts will be considered last.

Archeological speculations about Elizabethan playhouses began imperceptibly in the seventeenth century as
various painters, engravers and mapmakers mixed together old maps and views of London, correcting what
they thought faulty, supplying details from imagination,
and adding artistic flourishes as the spirit moved them.
As might be expected, pictures of playhouses, always
incorrect, steadily degenerated until by the eighteenth
century the lost theatres were being regularly represented
as twice as high as they were wide.[5] One of the few
eighteenth century investigators to speculate about interior
arrangements was Malone, who is generally credited with
inventing the theory that a curtained "inner stage" was

used for discoveries and short scenes.[6] In 1836 the German scholar and novelist Ludwig Tieck produced an inspired guess as to the features of the Fortune, but it was only a guess and not a reconstruction. Aside from a few wholly conjectural drawings the nineteenth century added little to earlier notions.

More knowledgeable attempts began early in this century with the reconstruction, among others, of Cecil Brodmeier. Although Brodmeier championed an unworkable theory about the alternation of scenes on inner and outer stages, he was among the first to make systematic use of the scanty evidence. Three years later, in 1907, the Archer-Godfrey reconstruction appeared. This collaboration between a playwright and an architect produced the first important (and still influential) example of what C. Walter Hodges once called an "old, poky hybrid of a mousetrap and a Tudor tea-garden ... " (Hodges 1947: 108) and went on to poke gentle fun at as the Merrie Englande school of decoration (Hodges 1959: 9). Nonetheless the reconstruction of William Archer and W. H. Godfrey froze the decoration and internal arrangements of the Fortune (and except for shape, all other playhouses) in the form they still usually take. This "ingle-nook nostalgia" school of Globes has included almost every scholar between Brodmeier and John Cranford Adams. The proponents of a half-timbered theatre incorporating various acting alcoves in the wall behind a platform stage currently constitute the orthodox believers.

In recent years, however, they have not gone unopposed. In 1940, two years before the publication of Cranford Adams' major statement of his theories, George F. Reynolds published the results of his examination of plays performed at the Red Bull (Reynolds 1940). The evidence they present, he said, casts serious doubts on the existence of an "inner stage." In 1944 George R. Kernodle made public a new theory concerning the ancestry of the Elizabethan public playhouse and suggested that Shakespeare's stage was baroque rather than Tudor.[7]

C. Walter Hodges, who had enlisted in the ranks of the
orthodox in 1947, joined the dissenters three years later
with the theory (vigorously supported by A.M. Nagler in
1958) that "discoveries" were managed with a booth or
pavilion on the stage rather than an alcove behind it. Drawing to some extent upon Kernodle's observations, Hodges
began designing baroque amphitheatres as exuberant as
those of Cranford Adams and his school were quaint.

In 1953, Leslie Hotson presented indications that
Elizabethan plays were performed with spectators on all
four sides of the stage and promised further documentation of his thesis. This was forthcoming in 1954, and in
1960, when Hotson proposed a wide platform stage with
the actors' tiring house underneath and a property dock
behind the back wall of the stage, surmounted by expensive
galleries in which sat the highest-paying spectators. Locations on the stage were indicated by scaffold "mansions"
in the medieval manner, and most important, the actors
addressed themselves primarily to those best seats behind
the stage.

At present there are four kinds of reconstruction. The
more conservative investigators advocate a Tudor playhouse containing a platform stage and an arrangement in
the back wall of a group of stages, galleries and windows.
Deviating from them somewhat are writers who recognize
the inner stage, but think it was merely a "discovery space,"
i.e. a small opening at the rear of the stage used for brief
tableaux rather than for extended scenes. Turning for
documentation to the booth stages of strolling players, a
third group supports the theory that a removable booth was
placed upon the stage during plays requiring a discovery.
And finally, Leslie Hotson advances evidence from Spain
and medieval England in support of the thesis that Elizabethan plays were acted in the round. As I hope to make
clear, none of these groups has an air-tight case, but on
the other hand, all of their theories are worth careful consideration.

With the reconstructions of the two oldest playhouses, the Theatre and the Curtain, we make the acquaintance of C. Walter Hodges. Hodges, an imaginative and seemingly inexhaustible investigator, has reconstructed all but one of the theatres we are concerned with—some of them two and three times. Before examining his reconstructions we must enter a caveat. First, Hodges is often more concerned with the spirit than the letter. He will sometimes draw a whole theatre in order to illustrate certain features, apparently filling in the remaining details freehand and from imagination. Secondly, realizing the absurdity of believing that all the playhouses came off an assembly line with interchangeable components, Hodges is likely to base one stage on one idea, and another on a second. For example, despite his advocacy of a pavilion discovery space, Hodges has not hesitated to provide some of the reconstructions in The Globe Restored with inner stages. Finally, although he scrupulously documents the features on which he is concentrating, Hodges spends little time explaining his selection and combination of less important stage appointments. Consequently it must be remembered that each reconstruction represents Hodges' conjectures at one particular time, and, moreover, that in my discussion of them I have often had to deduce those conjectures from the drawings alone.

Hodges' painting of Shoreditch (Hodges 1948: Frontispiece) shows the two earliest playhouses. The Theatre, in the foreground, is an octagonal building approximately forty by eighty feet in size, surmounted by a hut based on the De Witt Swan drawing, only with a rear extension over the thatched roof.[8] Two external stair housings are visible, one in each segment of the building immediately flanking the section directly opposite the stage. Directly behind the tiring house area is a one-story extension, apparently a service building of some sort. The only visible interior detail is the heavens roof, or "Hut," joined to the main building above the third gallery. (The "heavens," probably painted with stars, clouds, and even signs of the zodiac, was the projecting roof over the stage platform.)

The most interesting feature of this reconstruction is the pair of "jutties forwards." The Fortune contract says, in part: "All [three] Stories shall conteine Twelue foote and a halfe of lawfull assize in breadth throughoute, besides a juttey forwardes in either of the saide twoe vpper Stories of Tenne ynches of lawfull assize ... " A jutty (more often spelled "jettie" by Elizabethans) is simply the extension of an upper story out beyond the story immediately below it. The projection is supported by a cantilever arrangement.

First, what direction is "forwardes?" This of Hodges is the only reconstruction on which the jutties are outside the theatre; all other conjectures show them on the inside of the hollow playhouse, facing the yard. Ostensibly this usual arrangement would have afforded the gallery spectators some protection from the weather. But on the other hand, projecting upper stories were a common feature of Tudor houses, and as used on these buildings they usually faced the street. If they were so placed on theatres, they would have added to the rear of the upper galleries, thereby flattening (and hence, improving) the angles of vision from these locations. Conversely, jutties on the fronts of the galleries would have brought front-row spectators closer to the stage, with a consequent worsening of sight lines. Since the advantages and disadvantages of each location are roughly equal, it is interesting that so many reconstructions show jutties inwards.

The second problem concerns "either." Most investigators have assumed that the word means "both" here, although the O. E. D. also records "one or the other" as a common contemporary definition. All the juttied theatres we shall examine are provided with two projections.

The Curtain, partially obscured by intervening trees, is also octagonal with similarly positioned external stair housings, and its overall proportions are much the same. However, the hut is a truncated version of that in Hollar's 1647 view of the Second Globe, complete even to the peaked turret. Moreover, there are no visible jutties, and the building is not half-timbered.

Obviously, Hodges' intention was not to produce a careful reconstruction, but to design two playhouses by the eclectic combination of details from various sources.[9] It is the setting that is important here, and in its depiction of the road running north from Bishopsgate through Shoreditch, Hodges' view is excellent.

The next playhouse with which we must deal is the Swan, reconstructed by Hodges (Hodges 1953: 174) and by Richard Southern (Southern 1959). Hodges' drawing, again without much explanation, is based on the De Witt sketch. The best thing about this reconstruction is Hodges' attempt to make sense out of his evidence without distorting it in order to conform to any notion of what the playhouse ought to have contained. The tiring house façade is just as it appears in the sketch, only with the addition of an opening in the third story, an area concealed by the heavens in the De Witt sketch. The heavens itself is tiled. For the sake of symmetry the hut balcony on which De Witt's trumpeter appears (if he is a trumpeter) is given a mirror-image on the opposite side of the hut. The two great stage doors are the only entrances; Hodges has resisted the temptation to supply the stage with any discovery space, whether alcove or pavilion. Similarly, he has refused to enclose the stage with palings or hangings, since despite the need for entrances from belowstage the De Witt drawing shows the stage underpinnings unconcealed. It is regarding these supports that Hodges has made his most sensible deviation from his source. The supports in the De Witt drawing are peculiar to say the least. They are bigger than necessary and placed much too far forward to properly support the stage. Hodges has moved them back until they are directly under the great stage columns and hence carry the weight of the hut straight down to the ground. The rest of the stage is supported by smaller posts. The ingressi (entrances to the first gallery) are where De Witt put them and the exterior staircases are where Hollar

placed them on the Hope and the Second Globe. Each entrance is connected to a staircase by a short aisle behind
the seats of the first gallery. The main entrance is directly opposite the stage, a position justified by the fact
that none appears in the De Witt sketch, apparently because of the observer's position directly over it in one of
the galleries.

The only real defect in this reconstruction is the un-
easy connection between the gallery entrances and the stair-
wells. De Witt's ingressi are one third of the building
apart, separated by the section incorporating the stage
area, while the Hollar stair housings are in comparable
positions on the opposite side of the playhouse. Since the
two men drew different theatres, there is no reason to
follow both at once, connecting gallery entrance and staircase by a conjectural aisle. Logically, they should be
together, whether forward (following the De Witt sketch)
or toward the rear, (following Hollar). The latter position would create less of a traffic problem, since gallery
sitters would not have to cross much of the yard in order
to reach the entrances to the more expensive seats. In
addition, Hodges has not made much of an attempt to
solve the problem of sight lines, which in this reconstruction are not good.

These sight lines are the particular concern of Richard Southern, to whose reconstruction we now turn.
Southern's conjecture is also based on the De Witt sketch,
with dimensions calculated from the Fortune contract.
These dimensions are important to his argument, since
he maintains that a forty-three foot stage in a sixteen-
sided polygon (his modification of De Witt's round theatre)
would have taken up too much space and made sight lines
impossibly bad. The same stage in a square building such
as the Fortune would not have presented these problems.
It is his conclusion that in a polygonal playhouse whose
diameter is eighty feet (the outer dimension of the Fortune),
the stage can be no more than thirty-one feet wide
(Southern 1959: 24). This seems perfectly reasonable,

especially since this dimension is closer to the apparent
size of the stage in the De Witt drawing.

But Southern's concern for sight lines does not end
here. He has re-examined the Swan drawing and discovered that there are more support pillars between the
gallery rails and gallery ceiling than between the rails
and the floor, even above the two flights of ingressus steps
where there is nothing to support such pillars. His explanation is that half of the pillars shown (i.e. every other
one) were set halfway back in the gallery. Then, recalling
the various contract specifications of "partitions" for two-
penny "rooms," he conjectures that these dividers, like
those in eighteenth century theatres, were probably elbo-
high, so as not to obstruct the view, and were supported
by the front and middle pillars (ibid. 28). Now if the
gallery heights were like those in the Fortune contract,
there would have been head room for only four banks of
seats in the second gallery and two in the third. Therefore, the extra space, increased ten and twenty inches
respectively by the jutties, would have gone to waste.
Consequently, Southern conjectures that behind the "degrees" of the second gallery was a ceiling-high wall
pierced with entry doors. This wall, plus the elbow-high
section dividers supported by the middle columns, together formed the "rooms" mentioned (ibid. 28). The
narrow corridor behind the second gallery would have been
quite dark, and hence the windows seen in so many Bankside views would have been cut into the walls. The substantial area behind the benches on the top gallery might
have been a promenade (the hint for this is De Witt's label,
porticus) for dalliance, courtly or otherwise.

Ingenious as this theory is, it is not free from possible
objection. In the first place, there is at least one other
explanation for the extra pillars in the De Witt sketch:
perhaps the gallery rails were paled in and ornamented on
the outside with occasional decorative posts. This would
account for the blank area below the railings, and for the
relatively few pillars. It is also possible that Van Buchell

67

added the ingressi after he had drawn the amphitheatre.
Since he was working in ink, he could not erase the pillars he had drawn above the place where his steps (added,
significantly, without any perspective, in the plane of
the railing) should have been. In any case, De Witt (or
Van Buchell) was able to indicate perspective, even though
incorrectly. There is no indication in the sketch that every
other pillar was behind another. But even granting these
pillars and the half-partitions they conjecturally support,
there is no good reason for the back walls. They would
not have kept people out of the seats unless there had been
a guard at every door, they would have provided no privacy,
since the side walls adjoining them were only elbow-high,
and they would not have been structurally necessary in a
gallery only twelve feet deep (again the Fortune dimension).
And as a matter of fact, "room," according to the O. E. D.
could mean simply "place" or "location" without any con-
notation of enclosure. The only definite references we
have to room "walls" are not to the two-penny rooms but
to the small gentlemen's rooms. Like Hodges, Southern
has supplied De Witt ingressi and Hollar stair housings,
connected by an aisle.

Southern's reconstruction is noteworthy for three additional conjectures. Like Hodges, he decorates his
theatre in the baroque style typical of German and Flem-
ish-influenced buildings of the period. Unlike Hodges, he
hangs tapestries across De Witt's blank tiring house wall
to conceal a discovery space and covers the stage supports with a richly woven or painted cloth. To all these
conjectures there can be no serious objection, except
that De Witt's wall is so emphatically blank that I doubt
whether the Swan had a recessed discovery space. Finally, it might be noted that Southern has cooked the dimensions of his sketch of a performance at the Swan, in order
to make the playhouse seem more vast and magnificent
than his plans and elevations allow for.

Another drawing of the Swan, omitted above because
it is not actually a reconstruction, was made by Marjorie

and C. H. B. Quennell (Quennell 1919: II. 71). This sketch is well worth the reader's inspection because the artists have not interpreted the De Witt sketch, but merely redrawn it, translating the pictorial shorthand of the original into a more modern graphic idiom. Aside from concealing the stage supports and adding half-timbering to the hut, the Quennells have made only the most necessary compromises with the sketchiness and faulty perspective of their source. As an emendation of Van Buchell's draughtsmanship this drawing has much to recommend it.

Were we proceeding in chronological order, the First Globe would concern us now, but since it has been saved for last, we pass on to the Fortune, erected in 1600. The surviving builder's contract, which, as we have already seen, provides a number of important dimensions, has led to more reconstructions of this playhouse than of any other theatre except the First Globe.[10] We shall begin with the imaginary production of Ludwig Tieck, published in 1836.[11] This conjectured playhouse has been singled out A. M. Nagler because it shows a pavilion rather than an inner stage. Hodges uses it to point out that even in 1836 the German predilection for the baroque produced a decorative scheme that is closer to the original than most twentieth century reconstructions. Be that as it may, Tieck lacked some of the materials necessary for a documented reconstruction (the De Witt drawing had not been discovered) and so his playhouse has only curiosity value for us.[12]

Far more important is the joint reconstruction made by William Archer and Walter H. Godfrey in 1907 (Archer 1907. See plates one and two-left). This was the first detailed "scientific" reconstruction to attract wide notice, and it established a number of features that were to become conventional in most subsequent attempts. Godfrey, the architect who made the drawings, enthusiastically embraces the Tudor-pot decoration to which Hodges objects, and, more importantly, Archer postulates an inner stage seventeen feet wide and seven deep, flanked by doors set

at an oblique angle (ibid. 163). His evidence consists of
the need, obvious (to Archer) from a great many texts,
for a discovery space and a gallery above the stage built
in a wide, shallow bracket shape so that actors could stand
on one arm of it and look down into the inner stage. The
oblique doors were set into the similarly oblique façade
necessary to support these arms. Here, like many other
investigators, Archer assumes that his reading of texts
and stage directions is the only one possible. He notes
that the inner stage and oblique doors developed into the
Restoration-type proscenium with its extensive forestage
and proscenium doors (ibid. 166). This idea, not entirely
original with Archer, has been seized upon by later investigators, who have ignored the fact that the Restoration stage owed a great deal more to the court masque
stages and to Parisian tennis-court theatres than to the
public playhouse.

The architectural arrangements include some other
notable firsts. The elevation shows that Godfrey drops
the level of the yard two feet below ground level and
raises the stage only four feet above this pit. Hodges and
others have argued that a stage this low contradicts all
our evidence concerning Renaissance platform stages,
which were usually quite high, some of them as much as
seven or eight feet above the ground. Godfrey's galleries
are reached by three sets of stairs: one in each corner of
the stage end of the building and one directly opposite the
stage by the main entrance arch. This arrangement is
open to question. Unlike the other playhouses, the Fortune
was erected in a built-up section rather than in a field or
marsh near the Thames. Hence an unobstructed view of
the building from any distance whould have been impossible.
It seems logical, therefore, that the most impressive side
of the building, the stage and tiring house with its hut and
advertising flag (if these features were present) would
have faced the open street. Unless the audience filed
around the building to the rear, the entrances would have
been on the tiring house side of the building, as Hodges

has placed them in his reconstruction. As for the staircases themselves, the Fortune contract plainly indicates
that they were outside and attached to the building rather
than erected in the corners of it. But Archer dismisses
this evidence for external stair-housings with the incorrect statement that no view of any public theatre shows
any. Aside from the purely conjectural tiring house and
the misplacement of staircases and entrance, the Archer-
Godfrey reconstruction suffers from a number of less
important faults, among them the clumsy entrances to the
gallery stairs and the fact that the heavens is joined to
the stage at the floor of the third gallery, thereby decided-
ly interfering with the view from that location.

Despite these faults, this reconstruction is a sober
and conscientious attempt at archeology by a playwright
who knew a great deal about theatre and an architect who
was equally at home with building. The trouble is that
the features of this reconstruction were determined, not
by Elizabethan stage practices and building decoration,
but by early twentieth century notions of them. Playgoers
in 1600 did not yearn, consciously or unconsciously, for a
proscenium stage, nor by that date did builders decorate
large urban buildings as though they were cottages in the
Cotswold hills.

Before proceeding to the reconstruction of E. K. Chambers it should be noted that the handsomely rendered elevation and view of the Fortune made by A. Forestier for
the Illustrated London News (Forestier 1911) is an unacknowledged reproduction (with a few slight changes in the
patterns of the half-timbering) of the Archer-Godfrey
reconstruction. The only structural modification concerns the gallery heights, which do not follow the Fortune
contract. If the first gallery is taken to be twelve feet
high, as the contract requires, then the third seems to be
just under fourteen feet instead of nine.

In 1923, E. K. Chambers published diagrams of the
Fortune and the First Globe (which we shall come to anon.
Chambers 1923: III, 84-85). His examination of materials

is lengthy and careful, as usual, and the skeletonic reconstruction he proposes is conservative. Since he contents himself with reproducing the bare dimensions of the building, we can concentrate on his conjectured tiring house. Many of the playes he has scanned demand an upper acting platform of some kind, most probably a gallery flanked with windows. But Sir Edmund's main concern is with the discovery space, the necessity for which he proves at some length (Chambers 1923: III. 63-90). He wants a small, shallow place between two entrance doors (which are not oblique because the tiring house of a square theatre would probably have extended straight across one side) sufficient to contain the action which was unquestionably displayed there. In his opinion, thirteen by fifteen feet would have sufficed, since he does not believe, as Cranford Adams does, that lengthy or important scenes were staged "within." The radical feature of his reconstruction is the stage itself, which is shaped like a squat "T" with the cross, about twelve feet deep, and at the back of the stage against the tiring house, extending from one side wall to the other. The shank of the "T" is forty-three feet wide, as specified in the contract. Chambers also extends the tiring house area into the two sides of the building, so that the wide part of the stage touches the tiring house facade on three sides. By providing each extension with a door, Chambers creates two on-stage areas six by twelve feet each, on which gallants could have sat without hampering the movement of the actors or the view of the spectators in the yard and galleries. Chambers gives no plans for the upper galleries, but if this arrangement were duplicated above (perhaps with lords' rooms above the stage-sitters) the sight lines from the second and third tiers would have been similarly improved.

It is perfectly possible, of course, that a T-shaped stage was so standard that the Fortune contract did not need to mention it, but such an assumption, without any information that could even be construed as documentation for this conjecture is dangerous. Nonetheless,

Chambers' reconstruction is, on the whole, so simple and so cautious that it is difficult to resist. Anyone interested in stage essentials will profit from an inspection of his version.

From Chambers', we turn to the latest reconstruction of the Fortune, that of Hodges (Hodges 1953: 175). This reconstruction follows the specifications of the Fortune contract, so we need not concern ourselves with overall dimensions, except to note that Southern's point about sight lines is reinforced by the fact, obvious from Hodges' carefully executed view, that many spectators in the side bank of the top gallery would have been able to see little of the stage. The decor of Hodges' Fortune is more exuberantly baroque than that of his Swan, since the Fortune was a later and presumably fancier playhouse. Hodges' conjectured entrance arches, connected to the corner staircases noted previously, possess the additional advantage of using the six-foot-wide areas on either side of the stage as entrance aisles. But in suggesting that the arches were concealed in the angles of the building on the tiring house side, Hodges falls into Archer's error, forgetting that the contract unmistakably specifies external stair housings. It might also be noted that two triple flights of stairs within the building would have substantially diminished the tiring house area.

As for the stage house, the heavens and columns are taken over from the Swan drawing and the hut is a modification of the Globe hut in the Visscher panorama. The heavens is painted with cheerful stars and clouds surrounding a central opening for flying effects. The most interesting part of this reconstruction is the discovery space and its attendant features. Hodges has shown an inner stage of the conventional type (despite the fact that when he made this drawing he was an advocate of the pavilion stage), flanked by two sets of doors in the flat façade. These doors are surmounted by two matching pairs of window stage arches on the second level. The arches flank another inner stage which is galleried and

curtained. The resulting tiring house, though purely conjectural, is tastefully proportioned and not markedly at
variance with any information we have.

Turning the page in Hodges' book, we come upon the
next two theatres with which we must deal: the Hope and
the Second Globe, both erected around 1614 (Hodges 1953:
176-177). Both reconstructions are based on the Hollar
view of 1647, the Hope supplemented by the surviving
builder's contract and the Globe filled in with features
taken from John Webb's designs for the Cockpit theatre
(1632) and from the Schouwburg theatre, built in Amsterdam in 1658.[13] Hodges' drawings are more fanciful here,
because he has relatively less source material. The only
distinctive feature of the Hollar drawing is the Hope's pecul-
iarly peaked roof (it will be recalled that Hollar reversed
the names of the two theatres), and the Hope contract says
little more than that the playhouse was to have no stage
posts and a removable stage to facilitate the conversion
of the building to a bear ring. In most other respects it
was to be patterned after the Swan. Two boxes in the first
gallery were ordered for gentlemen. Hodges' contribution
(following a suggestion in Shapiro 1948: 34) is to connect
the two singular features of the sources: the peaked roof
and the unsupported heavens. Probably, he says, the
heavens was supported by an arrangement of beams rooted
in the roof. The odd peak was designed to permit these
long supports to project down and out over the stage area,
supporting the heavens as if by a sort of crane.

Hodges' Hope is a sixteen-sided polygon with three
galleries and no jutties. He is on reasonably firm ground
here, but the remainder of his drawing is more useful as
an impression of the playhouse than as a detailed reconstruction. Before a truly acceptable conjecture can be
made by anyone, a good deal of thought must be devoted to
the other modifications necessary in a multi-purpose
amphitheatre. The requirements of actors and animals
are different, despite opinions to the contrary. Actors
enter four to six feet from the ground on a trestle stage.

Animals enter at ground level, through doors that are
opened differently from those designed for humans.  The
tiring house would not have served as an animal pen, and
the kennels would never have done for property storage.
Arrangements for spectators would also have differed
somewhat since protection from the animals would have
been important to the spectators in the first gallery.  This
particular reconstruction is not a very impressive theatre
either.  The diameter of the yard is not more than about
forty feet and the width of the stage does not exceed twenty-
one.  Such a playhouse might have been built twenty years
earlier, but in 1614 it could not have remotely approxi-
mated the splendor of the Fortune and the newly rebuilt
Globe.  Nonetheless, in its explanation of the terms of the
contract and the odd roof shown by Hollar, Hodges' reconstruction is extremely valuable.

His reconstruction of the Second Globe embodies a
more radical conjecture:  that by 1614, the style of London playhouses was beginning to change in the direction of
the proto-proscenium stages exemplified by the Cockpit
and the Schouwburg in Amsterdam.  The highly complex
tiring house façade is designed in an assortment of full-
blown, concave curves, pierced again by inner and upper
stages, and flanked by no less than twelve entrances
(three in a row on each side of the inner stages) following
the curves of the tiring house.  On the evidence of the
Hollar view, the heavens and hut have been enlarged to the
point where the line of their façade is a diameter of the
circular building.  Details of the stage and the ubiquitous
jutties come from the Fortune contract.

Hodges' departure from tradition in the matter of the
tiring house needs some further investigation, but it is not
as disturbing as the proportions of his reconstruction as
a whole.  It is not difficult to calculate from the standing
figure in the drawing that the stage is not more than thirty-
five feet wide and is set in a yard less than forty-five feet
in diameter.  Considering Southern's demonstration that

a polygonal or circular theatre can contain less people than a square theatre of the same dimensions, it is odd that the round Globe should have been ten feet smaller than its rival the Fortune. However, it is possible that, considering the shift of emphasis to the "private" theatres, the King's Men were content to rebuild their public play-house without adding to the old pilings. Nonetheless, the Hollar view shows that the ratio of the Second Globe's diameter to its height-to-eaves was greater than three to one. If Hodges' galleries are laid out according to the Fortune contract, and his proportions indicate that they are, then the height-to-eaves of the reconstruction is thirty-five feet, producing a ratio of only two to one.[14]

Before proceeding to "synthetic" reconstructions of public theatres, we might note that the conjectures just dealt with are also synthetic, to the degree that recon-structions of any one theatre embody features deduced from evidence about other theatres or supplied from the investigators' imaginations.

Perhaps the first synthetic reconstruction to exert any influence on other investigators was that of Cecil Brodmeier (Brodmeier 1904. See plate two-right). Brod-meier's reconstruction is fairly primitive, but it is an attempt to resolve the two inescapable facts of the Swan drawing and the need for some kind of discovery space. The Swan drawing has puzzled every scholar whose work we have discussed so far because it shows a theatre ut-terly devoid of any facility for revealing the tableaux called for by a substantial number of plays. To supply an inner stage, Brodmeier conjectures a rear stage placed between the great heavens columns of the Swan. Solid walls (concealed by De Witt's angle of view) extend from each pillar to the tiring house wall. An arrangement of three curtains, one across each side wall and one across the open front, completes the inner stage. The actors played "outer" scenes before the closed front curtains while stage-hands set up properties for "inner" scenes behind them. When the closed area was needed, the curtains were drawn to disclose the interior. Brodmeier accepts the theory that to accommodate this system, Renaissance plays were composed of alternating interior and exterior scenes. Chambers and others have pointed out that such an arrangement would have rendered half the play totally invisible to half the audience and that threshold scenes (scenes played with some actors on the balcony and others on the apron) would have lost much of their point if played, according to Brodmeier's theory, in front of the closed "interior."[15] However, Brodmeier has received some support from each of two opposing schools. The pavilion of Hodges and A. M. Nagler is similar to Brodmeier's Hinterbühne, though a good deal more practical, and the "re-entry law" endorsed by Cranford Adams bears some resemblance to Brodmeier's alternating inner and outer scenes.

The reconstruction of Victor E. Albright (Albright 1909) attempts to elevate the Messalina vignette to the importance of the De Witt sketch. Albright discards the Swan sketch as unreliable and the frontispiece to The Wits as too late. The Roxanna vignette he accepts, but because it appears with an academic play, he prefers to base his reconstruction on the very similar Messalina drawing (ibid. 45). This sketch shows a tapered stage, so Albright tapers his, not down to twenty-four feet, as Cranford Adams suggests, but to fifteen, thereby producing an arrangement that would have served admirably for the opening scene of The Tempest, but would have been woefully inefficient for anything else (see plate three-left). He backs the second level gallery with brick, again following the vignette and caps the tiring house with a hut that appears to be a variation on the hut in the De Witt drawing, despite his rejection of De Witt as a source. Behind the "tarras" (gallery) is a large, curtained window instead of the inner stage we would expect to find, and the tarras itself is adorned with crenelations instead of a railing to provide a set-piece for scenes before fortified walls.[16] Albright conjectures a very substantial inner stage (ten by twenty-five feet), partly because of the inconceivability in 1909 of a stage without some kind of proscenium and partly because Albright subscribes to the "alternation" theory of staging espoused by Brodmeier (ibid. 116 ff).

This reconstruction is a careful attempt to fit the features of the Messalina vignette into a playhouse in which plays were staged with one scene on the outer stage and the next scene within. But since both the source and the theory are highly suspect, the reconstruction is correspondingly weak. J. Q. Adams has pointed out the risks involved in basing a reconstruction on a very late engraving by an unknown artist of meager skill who had about one square inch in which to work and who probably based his sketch on the Roxanna vignette (Q. Adams 1911). Of the four known drawings of theatre interiors, the Messalina vignette is probably the least valuable. And the alternation theory of staging is an invention based on a conception of theatre as depending to a great extent on the effects produced by "discovered" scenery. Albright's theory is outdated, but his book made a number of contributions to the study of stage conditions.[17]

The reconstruction of John Corbin is somewhat more conservative (Corbin 1911. See plate six-bottom).[18] For this rather eclectic design Corbin selects the dimensions in the Fortune contract, the columns in the De Witt drawing, the hut from the Visscher engraving and the decoration and oblique doors from the Archer-Godfrey reconstruction, with probably a bow to Albright, and combines all these elements in a reasonable if purely hypothetical theatre. The only compromise with the theatrical taste of 1911 appears in the tiring house façade, which is provided with two almost identical proscenium stages, one on top of the other. Corbin's only real gaffe is his conjecture that the term "heavens" meant "a cloud of canvas thrown out from the loft above the stage toward the top of the amphitheatre" to darken the stage for night scenes and effects such as storms.

Here, as with Albright, the theatrical techniques of the early twentieth century interfere with archeology. No director, even today, is anxious to present any play in flat daylight. Corbin did not see that the most convincing storm in Lear is within the king, not the playhouse.[19]

A reconstruction of a typical theatre was published in conjunction with an article by Milton Smith (Smith 1931: 38, 44). This design is completely conventional, except for the platform stage. Apparently accepting the correctness of the De Witt drawing, the artist has made the stage considerably deeper than it is wide. He has also tapered it in obvious imitation of the Roxanna and Messalina vignettes. Neither conjecture bears examination. We have had occasion to note the shakiness of the evidence for a tapered stage, and the Fortune contract specifies a stage much wider than it was deep. If we accept the theory (and there is strong reason for doing so) that the Fortune was patterned on the First Globe, then we are reasonably safe in assuming that the Globe's stage was also wider than it was deep. Perhaps some other playhouse had such a stage, but the evidence is far too weak (there is only the De Witt drawing with its patently faulty perspective) to permit its inclusion in a "typical" playhouse.

We have noted here and there that investigators such as Hodges and Southern advocate baroque decoration for Elizabethan public theatres. The next "typical" theatre represents an exploration in another direction: Allardyce Nicoll has published a drawing of a playhouse decorated in the Renaissance Italian manner (Nicoll 1927: 125. See plate four-top). This drawing shows a square theatre, half covered by an extensive heavens resembling a ceiling rather than a roof, surmounted by a hut based on the De Witt drawing. The single gallery stage is on the third level. At the tiring house the stage extends from wall to wall, but downstage it is tapered. Two flat doors flank a central opening on the first level and two more are set into the sides of the theatre where the stage joins the side walls. The center arch appears to be furnished with a perspective vista.

79

There is our clue. The entire reconstruction is laid out and decorated in the Palladian manner with niches full of bric-à-brac, carved lozenges and other decorations, and a high, narrow central arch for a discovery space. In support of this Italianate playhouse Nicoll says, "...Burbage, who was no illiterate or inartistic boor, may have been inspired by the example set at Vicenza. If this is so then the Theatre and the Globe represent attempts to reproduce in England the forms of a Roman playhouse." (Nicoll 1927: 123). That the Theatre was operating by August first, 1577, three years before construction on the Teatro Olimpico was begun and eight before it was completed is only one flaw in this theory. Even if we grant a less specific Italian influence, we can ask why Nicoll, or his artist, takes Chambers' risk by placing a wall-to-wall stage in a square theatre when the contract for the only known square playhouse specifies a stage that does not reach either wall? What is more, a forced-perspective vista requires considerable space (the central vista at Vicenza was over fifty feet deep), enough space to materially alter the shape of the building. Even if the London playhouse vistas had been more modest than their Italian models, they would have required a rear projection too distinctive to have been overlooked by all the engravers of maps and views.

Even if we grant that the stage-form and the vista are relatively minor matters, (the area behind the arch in the drawing might not even be a vista) Nicoll's conjectured Italian influence is open to question. The "classical" influences which spread outward from Henry VIII's Office of Works were not truly Italian, but French, usually French of the Fontainbleau School. In general, French decorative motives and techniques continued (always applied to a basic Tudor-Gothic design) into the 1560s, when they were gradually replaced by the methods and patterns brought in by artists from northern Europe. The "antic style" affected by late Tudor and Jacobean builders was a remote descendant of the styles of Michaelangelo and the Italian Mannerist architects of the first part of the seventeenth century. The Flemish artisans and pattern book engravers who relayed these Italian designs to England selected and emphasized not the fundamentals of their models, but the incidentals: the lozenges and entablatures, the filigree and the grotesques, and all the other paraphernalia of intricate and over-ornate decoration. The revered classical orders that had been borrowed from Serlio and the recently discovered Vitruvius were coarsened in their proportions and cheapened with busy, graceless fancywork. Not until Inigo Jones began to champion a more or less classical architecture did northern influence abate, and the so-called "Jacobethan" style (which was no style at all) did not completely die out until some years after the Restoration.[20] Professor Nicoll's theory is intriguing, but, published some years before the researches of George R. Kernodle called attention to this baroque influence, it attempts to merge Italian and English playhouse history many years before the two streams actually joined.

Kernodle's theories, which first aroused interest in baroque playhouse design, were accompanied by a playhouse reconstruction (Kernodle 1944: 152. See plate four-botton).[21] It is Kernodle's theory that the English public stages developed from the tableaux vivants and triumphal arches that had been popular for centuries, both in England and on the Continent. Consequently he has combined the customary features of reconstructed playhouses with elements drawn from arches, tableaux stages, and municipal theatres. The discovery space is notable for its pair of huge doors, which could have closed it completely for scenes taking place outside castles and city walls. For the same reason the upper stage (there is no tarras) is fronted with a battlement resembling that of Albright. The window stages, hung with the flags and banners so often seen in Kernodle's source pictures, are half a story lower than the upper stage. There is no third-level "musicians' room." The heavens is roofed with a vaulted rather than a gabled roof. There is

no strong evidence for this and the De Witt sketch contradicts it; but then the Swan was not the only playhouse in
London.  As reconstructions of tiring houses go, this one
is soundly reasoned.

The trouble is that the artist who lifted the decorations
out of their several contexts has combined them according
to a taste that is clearly neo-classical rather than baroque.
There can be no quarrel with the idea that tableaux stages
and triumphal arches were among the ancestors of the
public theatres, but the impression of joyfully tortured
magnificence given by these structures (for fine examples
of which see Hodges 1953:  142-147) is far different from
that of Kernodle's quietly elegant conjecture.  Some of
Hodges' more ebullient designs are probably closer in
feeling at least, to the originals.

If Hodges and Kernodle agree to a great extent on the
decor of the playhouses, they differ on the subject of antecedents.  Where Kernodle links the public stages to
tableaux vivants and festival arches, Hodges is inclined
to trace them back to the booth stages of wandering theatrical troupes, which had been touring England and the
Continent in great numbers for more than two centuries
before the erection of the first English playhouse.  The
portable platforms on which these companies acted were
customarily supplied with a booth in the rear in which the
actors changed costumes and from which they made their
entrances onto the high trestle stage.  The different
genealogies are important because each leads to a particular conception of the discovery space in the London public
theatre.  Whereas representations of tableaux stages and
triumphal arches usually display a central arch framing
a recessed and often curtained area, pictures of booth
stages suggest the use of the tiring booth as a pavilion.
This is Hodges' contention:  losing its function of tiring
house, the booth evolved into a pavilion at the back of the
platform stage, but in front of the tiring house wall
(Hodges 1953:  34-61).[22]  Pavilions were used for
discoveries and for short scenes requiring a small en-

closed space: tents, tombs and the like. The pavilion roof was used for scenes played "aloft." This arrangement, says Hodges, is not only more consistent with the antecedents of the London playhouses but also brings much of the action out of the low, cramped cubby to which traditional reconstructions have relegated it. Hodges' theory has been strongly seconded by A.M. Nagler (Nagler 1958: 26-31).

There are further arguments for this tent. For one thing, London companies still traveled, and when they did so they must necessarily have used booth stages. Moreover, the very bareness of the tiring house wall in the De Witt sketch suggests that a booth of some kind was placed on the stage in the many cases when plays required three separate entrance doors. A pavilion could have been placed before a traverse covering both stage doors. Entrances through these doors would have been made through slits in the traverse, and the booth would have been both discovery space and third entrance (Nagler 1958: 49-51). The fact that the De Witt drawing shows no such arrangement can be explained by the fact, suggested by M. Holmes and amplified by Nagler, that De Witt did not sketch a performance but a rehearsal (Holmes 1956; Nagler 1958: 10-11). The curtains and booth had not been set up. Finally, Thomas Platter, attending a play at the Curtain during his travels in England, 1599, described in his journal a scene in which an Englishman, "went [or climbed] into the tents [or tent]" of a German to make off with a disputed woman.[23] Professor Nagler points to two instances in which contemporary Germans from Platter's Allemanic language area used Zelt in unmistakable reference to stage mansions, that is, to pavilions (Nagler 1958: 30-31).

The trouble with this theory is that each argument can be countered by another. Regarding the development of the discovery space, it has already been pointed out that Kernodle has considerable evidence leading to the conclusion that tableaux stages rather than booth stages were the ancestors of the public theatres. The Elizabethan

stage, as W. F. Rothwell has noted, was protean to say the
least, and actors were accustomed to adapting their performance techniques to the conditions in which they found
themselves. Thus, the existence of booth stages on the
roads of England does not guarantee their presence in the
permanent city theatres. There is no contemporary representation of a pavilion in a theatre, and no unmistakable
allusion to one. There is no reason to doubt that Platter
meant "pavilion" when he said "Zelt," but was he referring
to Professor Nagler's centrally-placed, semi-permanent
discovery space, or to a mansion: a special set-piece
placed somewhere on the stage? Nagler notes that actual
tents were sometimes used (as in Richard III), and the
scene Platter described involved a German warrior, who
might be expected to fall asleep in an actual tent. Similarly,
Thomas Dekker's reference (cited in Nagler 1958: 50) to
the gallant, creeping "... from behind the Arras ... " does
not specify whether these draperies covered the entire
back wall, as Nagler suggests, or whether they merely
concealed a recessed discovery space. It is true that the
De Witt drawing shows no discovery space and that such
an area would have been required for many plays, but a
conjecture designed to supply this space in the Swan need
not be extended to other playhouses.

Finally, the pavilion is not much more practical,
theatrically, than the alcove it is designed to replace.
Hodges objects to the alcove because action taking place
within it would have been remote from the audience. But
substituting a pavilion moves the action forward by only
eight feet or so, hardly a significant improvement on a
platform with a depth comparable to the Fortune's twenty-
seven-odd feet. The small, dark enclosed space is not
dispensed with, but only moved out so that it cannot be as
easily reached from the tiring house by actors and stage
hands. The pavilion stage theory is well argued and sub-
stantiated by enough evidence to lead us to suspect that
some theatres, especially the Swan, might have employed
such an arrangement, but this evidence does not warrant

84

the assumption that a pavilion was part of the "typical" stage.

As for the running debate between advocates of Tudor and baroque theatre decoration, this is not easily settled either. On the one hand, the Theatre, the First Globe, the Fortune, the Hope, and, therefore, presumably all the other amphitheatres were built with timber frames and wattle-and-daub wall construction. This traditional building technique lent itself easily to wall panels of decorative half-timbering, while large stone buildings were more likely to be bedizened with "antic style" ornaments. On the other hand, this newer decoration was "modern," intricate, cheerful, and brash—exactly the qualities one might expect to find in a public amphitheatre of the time. It was well-established in triumphs, pageants, and other theatrical spectacles, and was gaining ground in actual theatres in the Low Countries across the Channel. Moreover, since this baroque decoration was always an overlay rather than an integral part of a building, it could have been applied to wood construction as easily as to stone. Considering the frequency with which London theatres were praised (and damned) for their unusually impressive splendor, it is probably safe to conjecture baroque decoration garnishing Tudor construction.[24]

Despite the fact, pointed out by Professor Nagler (Nagler 1958: 18), that more than half of Shakespeare's plays received their first performances in theatres other than the Globe, Burbage's Bankside theatre has always been identified with his most illustrious playwright. Consequently, many "reconstructions" of the First Globe have been perpetrated in defiance of the unfortunate fact that almost no contemporary evidence for any of its features is extant. Actually, "reconstructions" of the First Globe are no more reprehensible than designs of "typical" playhouses, but it is too bad that those who have read and been convinced by such fantasies have gone forth to spread the gospel of what is wholly a revealed religion.

The first of these that we need deal with is the painting of A. Forestier, depicting a performance of <u>Henry IV Part One</u> (Forestier 1910; and in Hodges 1953: 129). Forestier's painting shows an immense round theatre surrounding a relatively small stage, which is raised a good six feet from the yard. Details of the heavens, columns and hut are from De Witt, Visscher et al., and the tiring house follows that of Archer and Godfrey fairly closely. The theatre itself is almost devoid of decoration, in accordance with the belief that Shakespeare's stage was a primitive, rough-hewn affair, and the hut is finished in the inevitable half-timbering. The painting has no new hypotheses to offer, but as an early and fairly competent attempt to give an impression of a performance in an Elizabethan playhouse it is worth examining.

The reconstruction of G. Topham Forrest is interesting in that it relies on the Hollar engraving for many of its exterior details (Forrest 1921: see plate five). The heavens, hut, and tiring house are fairly conventional, and the inner stage is a modest twelve feet wide. Where the reconstruction departs from orthodoxy it is not too successful. The heavens is arranged so that no flying effects would have been possible. The stage is only twenty-four feet wide by twenty feet deep, with the heavens columns at the front corners and a strongly convex forward edge. Thus Forrest's stage is roughly two-fifths the size of the Fortune's, and his convex front and stage columns contradict the De Witt drawing, even though the heavens supported by these columns is based directly on the Swan sketch. His auditorium also presents difficulties. Reasoning that, since it was built to compete with the Globe, the Fortune must have exceeded the older theatre in size, Forrest plans a Globe that is just under seventy feet in total diameter, with a yard no more than forty feet across. Taking a hint from Archer and Godfrey, Forrest drops his yard a good foot below ground level, a conjecture dubious enough in the case of the Fortune and fairly improbable when transferred to a Bankside theatre "flank'd with a ditch and forc'd out of a marish." The stage in this yard is only three feet high, contradicting all the known evidence on this matter, requiring a below-stage excavation of four feet and bringing the total depth below ground level to five feet. But if the height of the stage would have created bad sight lines for standees, the arrangement of galleries would have imposed worse conditions on the sitters. Forest borrows the Fortune gallery heights for a theatre ten feet smaller and provides no seat risers in the first gallery, only one in the second and two in the third. The angle of view from the front of the third gallery to the front of the platform opposite is about sixty degrees. A spectator in the back of the same gallery opposite the stage would have been unable to see any of the platform.

Two features worth more careful consideration are the shape of the theatre and the location of stairs and entrances. Unlike Hodges and Southern, who are forced to connect De Witt's yard steps with Hollar's stair-wells by a corridor behind the first gallery seats, Forrest has placed the two together in the location indicated by Hollar. This move simplifies the entrance arrangements, and relieves congestion in the yard. Forrest was also the first to effect the compromise between round and polygonal playhouses later adopted by Hodges, Southern and others: his playhouse is a sixteen-sided polygon, close enough to circular to be shown as such on some maps and views, but composed of more easily worked straight timbers.

More concern for sight lines is shown in the reconstruction of Joseph Quincy Adams (Q. Adams 1923: facing 284, 286, 288. See plate six-top). The tiring house area is conventional, with the exception of the heavens, which like that of Nicoll, is a ceiling rather than a roof. Another innovation is the theatre roof, which is single-gabled. It is impossible to compute the dimensions of Adams' Globe, since he provides no scale, includes no figure in his elevation, and does not follow the Fortune contract in his gallery heights. His galleries are lower than the Fortune's, a difference that flattens and therefore improves the angles

of vision from the upper galleries. If Adams' first gallery
is taken to be twelve feet high (like the lowest Fortune
gallery) then his second and third galleries are ten-and-
one-half and just under eight feet respectively, rather than
eleven and nine feet. To further improve sight lines, the
top gallery is provided with only two banks of seats compared to three each for the lower galleries. Unfortunately,
this concern for sight lines does not extend to the sides of
the galleries. The end walls of the tiring house are set at
right angles to the sections of the octagon immediately
adjoining the stage. Consequently, half of the audience in
the first gallery bays would have been unable to see into
the inner stage, and one fourth of them could have seen
only half of the platform.

We need not spend much time on E. K. Chambers' reconstruction of the First Globe, since it is merely his
Fortune, transformed into an octagonal theatre (Chambers
1923: III; 75). His design bears out Southern's observation that to equal the capacity of the square Fortune, the
round or polygonal Globe would have had to possess greater
overall dimensions. If the two playhouses were absolutely
identical, except for overall shape, the Globe, in Chambers'
reconstruction, would have contained approximately 275
square feet less yard area.

In 1942, John Cranford Adams published what is
probably still the most influential reconstruction of the
"Globe" theatre (C. Adams 1942).[25] He had previously
published a reconstruction based partially on that of
Joseph Quincy Adams, but his major statement is considerably different from this first attempt.[26] We shall deal
only with the second reconstruction. As has been intimated
above, there have been serious objections to this reconstruction, the most important of which must be aired here.
First, the various components of Adams' playhouse have
been tailored to conform with the theory that Elizabethan
staging involved almost as much use of various "inner"
and "upper" acting areas as of the platform stage. Secondly, the evidence adduced to document these components

is usually inconclusive and occasionally misapplied. Moreover, the conclusions regarding almost all the features of
Adams' playhouse are presented as incontrovertibly proved,
when in fact, they are based on Adams' theory of staging
and then on conjecture.

Before substantiating these objections we must note
the more important features of this reconstruction. Adams'
Globe is an octagonal building with a single entrance opposite the stage, connected by two exterior passageways
with the stair housings, placed one against each adjoining
section of the building. The tiring house is conventional
and the stage (exactly twenty-nine by forty-three feet) is
tapered. The yard is fifty-eight feet across the total
width of the playhouse is eighty-four feet (C. Adams 1942:
21. See plates ten, eleven and twelve).

The objections to Adams' theory of staging have been
amply stated elsewhere, and hence a summary is all that
is needed. According to Adams, as much as half the action
in many Elizabethan plays was staged in one or another of
the specialized acting areas rather than on the platform.
In King Lear, for instance, six of the twenty-six scenes
take place "above," four occur on the inner stage, four are
given on the inner and platform stages combined, and
twelve are played on the platform alone (C. Adams 1948).
Irwin Smith, who supports Adams' reconstruction, lists
the kinds of scene which would have been played in just
one of the supplementary acting areas: the inner stage:

> Lower-level scenes which involve discoveries.
> Lower-level scenes which involve the use of
> properties.
> Scenes in which a person knocks on a door, or
> is descried offstage, before entering.
> Scenes which refer to a door or stairway as
> leading to rooms above.
> Scenes in which a large group of persons is
> seated informally, such as a senate, parliament,
> council, or the like.
> Scenes in which ghosts or apparitionse rise to

the inside of a room, tent, or cave.

Generally speaking, all indoor scenes at ground level, particularly where a part of the stage is supposed to be in and the rest out.

Outdoor scenes which require specific localization or properties. (I. Smith 1956: 107-108. His italics).

This placement of large portions of every Elizabethan play ignores the psychology of theatre in general and Elizabethan audiences in particular. To assume that all scenes located "indoors" had to be played in a box is to mis-evaluate the mentality of the audience. Where the spectators demanded realism was not in background but in theatrical effect. Henslowe was obliged to lay out enormous sums for magnificent costumes and maintain a property room full of ingenious devices for spectacular beheadings, disappearances and so-forth. But Shakespeare and his fellow playwrights customarily wrote battle scenes for less than twenty men and no one but a few aesthetic purists objected. And if "asia of the one side and Afric of the other" failed to destroy the illusion for any but Sir Philip Sidney, it is presumptuous of modern scholars to assume that a tavern scene could not have been played on the open platform.

Moreover, the relegation of so many scenes to inner and upper stages generates additional mistakes. Adams spends a great deal of time adducing stage directions to prove the existence of various doors, windows and hangings inside his inner stage (C. Adams 1942: 167-228), but his arguments have weight only if it is accepted that the scenes he cites were written to be performed in this "study."

And as for the psychology of theatre in general, no experienced theatrical company of any age using any stage would relegate numerous, lengthy, and important scenes to a dark, remote recess at the back of the stage. The downstage area of any stage is the best place for effective presentation; "distance" as an artistic principles is aesthetic, not physical.[27]

The second major objection to Adams' reconstruction regards his documentation. It would be impossible, here,

to examine every one of his conjectures, since he enumer-
ates, describes and precisely locates practically every
feature of his playhouse but the sanitary facilities.  But
we can select some of the components previously noted
and check his evidence for them.

First, Adams is certain that the Globe was octagonal.
According to his survey of maps and views showing the
Bankside, only the Visscher and Hollar panoramas are
worth considering.[28]  The Hollar view is dismissed as
being "of negligible value", because it was engraved in
Amsterdam three years after the Globe had been torn
down (C. Adams 1942: 4).  But the existence of a pre-
liminary sketch indicates that Hollar drew the theatres
on the spot.  Adams further argues, without presenting
any evidence, that the theatres in the view bear no resemblance to descriptions of the Second Globe and the
Bear Garden, and he uses this unsupported assertion to
deny the generally accepted theory (put forth in Braines
1921 and elsewhere) that Hollar mistakenly reversed the
names of the two playhouses.  Adams bases his argument
for an octagonal Globe squarely on the Visscher drawing
which, "in beauty, in completeness of detail, and in skil-
ful execution... surpasses any other seventeenth century
view of London" (ibid. 7).[29]  After a painstaking analysis,
I. A. Shapiro has concluded from the many gross blunders
in this view that Visscher certainly did not draw the Bankside from observation and probably never even visited
London (Shapiro 1948: 27-28).  Of course, even if the
Visscher view is accepted, the fact that it was made
around 1616 presents difficulties if it is to be used as
evidence for the First Globe; so Adams states (again without explanation) that a slight variant which exists in a
unique copy in the Folger Library, was the original view,
made "1604-1614," and that the 1616 view is a copy by
Hondius (C. Adams 1942: 7).  But it is obvious from a
comparison of the two versions that the British Museum
copy (1616) is the original from which the undated Folger
version was taken.

Having stated his case for the octagonal shape of the First Globe, Adams then computes its dimensions. His reasoning is as follows: since the Fortune galleries were twelve feet deep (plus six inches of outer wall) and since carpenters preferred modular construction (whereby as many members of the frame and even sections of the building as possible have the same dimensions) we can assume that the Fortune galleries were composed of square bays twelve feet on a side, plus three half-bays seven by twelve feet each. If these dimensions are transferred to the octagonal Globe, then each section would contain two bays twelve feet each across the front, making each side twenty-four feet wide from the center of one corner pillar to the center of the next. An octagon of these dimensions would have an inner diameter of fifty-eight feet, encouragingly close to the Fortune's fifty-five feet, and the outer diameter (assuming the same gallery depth as in the Fortune) would be eighty-four feet (ibid. 21). Now, if the stage extended between the centers of the midposts of the galleries immediately flanking the tiring house section, it would be be forty-three feet wide, exactly the size of the Fortune stage. Since forty-three feet is too odd a figure to be coincidental, it is obvious that the Fortune stage was copied directly from the Globe's. Aside from the questionable assumption that this kind of close reasoning is valid where the evidence is as vague as this, Adams' proof is based on two conjectures: first that the Fortune was divided into fourteen, twelve-foot bays and three seven-foot bays. An equally probable arrangement might consist of five, eleven by twelve foot bays in each gallery and a twelve by twelve bay in each corner. These corner bays would not have any side facing the yard, and so their slightly greater size would not be noticed. All fifteen visible gallery units would be identical, and hence, more symmetrical than Adams'. Adams also assumes that the Globe bays were exactly as deep as the Fortune's. But these assumptions are not of prime importance, because, as the sharp-eyed reader has doubtless noticed, fifty-eight feet (the width of the yard) plus twenty-five feet (the combined depths of the galleries, including twelve feet of space and six inches of wall in each) is not equal to eighty-four feet, but to eighty-three. Moreover, a stage extending across the tiring house bay to the center of the midpost of each adjoining bay is not forty-three feet wide, but forty-one. The Fortune and Globe stage widths are not identical, and Adams' proof collapses.[30]

Unfortunately, we lack the space to consider any other features of this reconstruction. Adams' conjectures are so ingeniously reasoned that they require almost as much space to refute as to state. We must be content to note that many of his components, notably the location of the entrance and staircases, the excavated yard, the shape of the stage and the tiring house with its various acting areas, are vulnerable to objections. Perhaps it seems unfair to subject Adams to cross-examination on fine points while passing only the most general judgments on the other scholars whose reconstructions are no better. But unlike most other investigators, Adams presents us with fine points and presents them as proved once and for all. For instance, on page three of his book he announces, "I shall proceed to the builder's contracts which show that the [Globe] playhouse measured eighty-four feet between outside walls, thirty-four feet high to the eaves-line, and fifty-eight feet across the interior yard," (C. Adams 1942: 3). As we have seen, these contracts show nothing of the sort, and would not do so, even if Adams had not made a mistake in his calculations. As long as Adams insists that demonstrations based on unverified assumptions constitute proof, he must expect the caviling over specific points from which other, less positive scholars are exempt.

At this point the contribution of Irwin Smith should be explained. In 1956, Mr. Smith, who had collaborated with Adams on the model now in the Folger Library, published a book (I. Smith 1956) containing complete working drawings of this model. Although he subscribes to Adams' reconstruction, Smith is well aware that his partner's arguments are not as conclusive as they seem. His more moderate stand on the same issues is well worth comparing to Adams'; and his book contains invaluable reproductions of maps and views, along with welcome information regarding Tudor building techniques.

A final note on Adams' reconstruction concerns a modification made between 1942 and 1950. In 1947 Hodges suggested that Adams' reconstruction might be improved structurally and aesthetically by the addition of arches anchored to the stage columns and to the tiring house, thereby providing extra support for the heavens. (Hodges 1947). These arches were added to the reconstruction when it took concrete form as a model. This suggestion by Hodges marks his first venture into reconstructions. In the same article he proposes a second modification of Adams' stage. Hodges would like to extend the stage to the sides of the building at the rear, thereby getting rid of awkward waste space and providing the gallants with a place to sit without obstructing the view. This, of course, is the arrangement conjectured by E. K. Chambers in his reconstructions of 1923.

A year later Hodges published a detailed reconstruction of the Globe (Hodges 1948: 62-63. See plate seven)[31] We need not spend any time on the details of the tiring house area since the key accompaning the drawing supplies all necessary information. But some features of the building deserve special attention. For one thing, Hodges has followed Forrest in placing the stair housings directly behind the ingressi, a location he abandons in his 1953 reconstruction of the Swan. Moreover, he establishes two substantial entrance arches flanking the stage and includes a number of interesting conjectures regarding the usually ignored area inside the tiring house. Most instructive of all is his arrangement of seat banks in the galleries. It is clear from the drawing that four banks in each gallery would have been too many to permit even moderately good sight lines. Every spectator in the galleries opposite the stage could have had some view of

the tiring house area, but the downstage section of the
platform would have been completely invisible to many.
Taken together, Hodges' 1948 Globe and Southern's 1959
Swan perfectly illustrate the problem of sight lines. Southern's galleries, contrived to insure the best possible view
of the stage, waste so much space that no theatre manager
would be content with them, and Hodges' arrangements,
designed to use all the space in the galleries, provide such
a poor view of the stage that no spectator would be happy
to sit in them. All in all, however, Hodges' 1948 reconstruction of the Globe is a conservative and skillful blend-
ing of the information at hand with the more sensible earlier reconstructions.

It might be profitable here, to disregard chronological
order for a moment, in order to compare Hodges' 1948
reconstruction with his latest one, made ten years later
(Hodges 1958).[32] Like his early conjecture, Hodges' 1958
reconstruction shows a sixteen-sided theatre with a rectangular stage, and decorated in an intricately baroque
manner. There are, however, three important changes.
First, Hodges 1958 is based more closely on the De Witt
drawing. The belowstage area, enclosed, in Hodges 1948,
with wooden palings, is treated in much the manner of the
Hodges Swan reconstruction: the great stage columns
continue down to ground level, and are supplemented by
smaller posts. Cloth "hangings" are used to conceal them
from the audience. The hut is closer to De Witt's, although Hodges has placed an extra turret above it, and
the second level of the tiring house is a gallery fronted
with a series of arches reminiscent of De Witt's gallery.
Finally, Hodges has perhaps too slavishly followed his
sources by again placing his gallery entrance stairs in the
positions of De Witt's ingressi while putting his external
staircases two sections farther back, where Hollar indicated them in his Long View of 1647.

Hodges has adopted Southern's section divisions,
placement of gallery seat banks, corridor behind the second gallery seats and promenade back of the third. This

modification goes far toward solving the problem of sight
lines, but again, a good deal of space is wasted.

But the most important feature of this reconstruction
is the discovery space. Hodges 1948 shows a wide, rather
shallow opening in the tiring house façade – a full inner
stage. In 1950 he proposed the pavilion stage, and maintained this position in his most exhaustive treatment of
the subject, Hodges 1953. But the opening in this latest
tiring house is a true "discovery space:" a relatively
narrow, curtained opening flanked by two stage doors.
Having swung from conservative to radical positions,
Hodges has now taken the middle of the road. The faults
of this reconstruction are relatively minor, and in its
closeness to sources, its attention to sight lines and its
conservatism regarding controversial features, it is
probably the most useful conjecture yet made.

The next reconstruction to concern us was published
by F. E. Halliday (Halliday 1956: 83. See plate three-
right). In a round playhouse Halliday has set a rectangular
stage backed by a tiring house based, to some extent, on
the De Witt Drawing. The flat façade contains two doors
and supports a long gallery. A discovery space covered
by curtains has been added, and the heavens has been
raised to show a third level, pierced by what seems to be
a long, low window stage with smaller windows on either
side. The only departures from convention are two doors
into the yard, one on either side of the stage.[33] The hut
resembles that of the Globe in the Visscher panorama.
No dimensions are given, though it is possible to compute
that the stage is roughly thirty-five to forty feet wide,
and no explanation accompanies the drawing. Included
here because it is called the First Globe, Halliday's reconstruction is obviously a free, though perfectly sensible
impression of a "typical" public playhouse.

By far the most radical theory to be treated in this
paper is Leslie Hotson's contention that in the public
theatres as at court, Elizabethan drama was played in the
round (Hotson 1960. See plates eight and nine).

In Shakespeare's "wooden O" the wide, shallow stage (resembling the Fortune's twenty-seven and one half by forty-three feet) formed the roof of the tiring house, which was located underneath it where most reconstructors place the trap area. At both sides of this stage, two-story "houses" were erected and subdivided into rooms. These houses consisted of wooden frames supporting platforms about six and one half feet above the stage. Each room was enclosed by four draw-curtains; the upper levels were connected with the lower by stairs, and the lower communicated in the same way with the tiring house belowstage. Where we would expect to find the tiring house, we see instead the highest-paying spectators, sitting in the galleries protected by the heavens from sun, wind and rain. The stage sitters deployed themselves on stools across the front wall of the stage house, behind which was a large property dock, used also for mass entrances and exits.

It was to the elite spectators on and behind the stage that the actors customarily addressed themselves. The "penny stinkards" in the yard and the sun-blasted sitters in the galleries behind them were perforce content to stare at the backs of the actors, since their position allowed them to ogle the gentry at the same time. Those in the side galleries peered through the mansions at both ends of the stage.

The performance of a play was roughly as follows: masked "stage-keepers" manipulated the curtains shrouding the mansions. When an actor was to enter, he climbed from the basement tiring house up through a trap to the interior of a closed house. On cue he would be "discovered" by the stage-keepers, or else part the curtains and enter the main acting area. In either case, all four curtains would then be drawn so that those spectators sitting or standing behind the house could see the action on the main playing area. To make an exit, the actor would either return to a closed house, of if playing the scene in a "mansion", he would be masked by the drawing of the curtains. Again, either way, he would descend into the tiring house below to await his next cue.

97

This rather bald summary is inescapable, because Hotson's major statement of this theory is a fascinating and complex book, full of quotations, citations, impressionistic re-creations of performances, truculent sallies at other scholars, appendices and divers extraneous matter, all of which makes the documentation of any brief resumé exceedingly difficult.[34] The discussion to follow is confined to the three most important conclusions drawn from his investigation: first, the tiring house was under the stage. Secondly, the acting areas usually supplied by scholars as inner and upper stages were scaffold houses at each side of the platform. Finally, the actors played in the round, concentrating their attention on the high-paying spectators sitting "behind" the stage under the heavens.

Hotson makes his case for the subterranean tiring house as follows: first he establishes at some length the great popularity of the English pageants which began in the Middle Ages and continued up to the eighteenth century (Hotson 1960: 61-67). Then he shows that Spanish pageants, drawn about on carros like English pageant-houses, were provided with dressing rooms underneath the stage (ibid. 67-78). His documentary link between the English carts and the Spanish dressing rooms is Archdeacon Robert Rogers' description of the Chester pageant-wagons as two storied (ibid. 62-63). Unfortunately Archdeacon Rogers' account must be viewed with considerable suspicion since it was written, not by himself, but by his son David at least thirty-four years after the last performance at Chester. David Rogers, who was hostile to the pageants anyway, committed a number of other blunders in his account, as F.M. Salter has pointed out (Salter 1955: 54-55).

Nor is Hotson justified in limiting the ancestry of the Elizabethan public stage to the amateur craft cycles. The professional companies who eventually built the London playhouses customarily employed the pavilion stages described by Hodges.[35] There is no reason for replacing

these booths and platforms with Hotson's carros. There
is no indication that actors appeared from belowstage except in the case of special effects. The only known views
of theatre interiors show rear entrances only. Hotson,
who frequently calls upon scholars to accept labels at
face value, is forced to translate De Witt's "mimorum
aedes" ("actors' house") into a property dock from which
large groups of players occasionally entered (Hotson 1960:
90).[36]

A tiring house under the stage would have been hellishly
inconvenient. Hotson notes the Fortune contract's speci-
fication of windows in the tiring house, points out the peculiar stage supports in the De Witt drawing, and says they
are one and the same (ibid. 91). This connection seems
entirely unwarranted, but even if these vague rectangles
were windows, the press of "understanders" in the yard
would have blocked out the little light thus admitted.
Moreover, such a room would have been uncomfortably
low-ceilinged (unless the stage were eight feet high or the
ground excavated to well below the Bankside water-table)
and severely cramped by the extensive underpinnings
necessary to support a platform roughly twenty-five by
forty feet in size.[37] Removing the Hope's stage for bear-
baiting would have been an enormously complex task—in
fact an impossible task if the yard underneath were excavated. None of these objections proves that the tiring
house could not possibly have been beneath the stage, but
together they make the possibility highly unlikely. And
since Hotson's evidence for his conjecture is unsatisfactory, we cannot accept his theory.

Hotson's arguments for mansions at the ends of the
stage are similarly impractical. He has performed a
valuable service in bringing forcibly to our attention the
large body of evidence indicating the use of houses and
set pieces on the public stage, but his arrangement of
them will not bear scrutiny.[38]

First, these mansions are impractical from the point
of view of the stage carpenter who would have had to build

them. They are two stories high, and, though expected to support at least six people per unit (as in the tomb scene in Antony and Cleopatra), they are shown completely bare of any cross-bracing or other support. (Bracing, of course, would have contributed to the forest of timbers between the side galleries and the playing area.) Hotson says the uprights would have been set in sockets in the stage floor, but this would not have increased the safety of the superstructure. Moreover, Hotson's mansions would have been a decided nuisance to the actors. Climbing in and out of holes in the floor is difficult to manage quickly under any circumstances, let alone in theatrical costume. The supernumeraries performing the show of kings in Macbeth, for example, would have found scurrying around belowstage and scrabbling up steep ladders into cramped chambers no easy task. Most important, the audience would have objected to these houses because they would have seriously hampered vision. Hotson's structures would have required posts, platforms and curtains, not to mention incidental properties and set pieces within. Stairs and ladders would have poked through. The curtains alone (omitted from most of the drawings in Hotson's book) would have obscured as much as a foot at each corner of each house. Moreover, according to Hotson's theory of staging, they would have been constantly opening and closing as the stage-keepers prepared rooms for various scenes and concealed entrances and exits. Imagine a performance of Antony and Cleopatra staged in this manner. At almost every point of the play at least one booth would be closed, blocking the view of one or two hundred spectators.

But, says Hotson, the gallery sitters knew what they were in for; the plays were staged primarily for the lords and gentles sitting above the "property dock" and on the stage. The company addressed itself to those spectators who provided the most revenue. But when viewed in the light of the De Witt drawing this statement does not make sense. Aside from the fact that De Witt has clearly

labelled the far part of a lower gallery (the worst seats in
Hotson's Globe) "orchestra" ("Place for the senators"),
the gallery above the Swan stage could not possibly have
yielded enough admissions money to permit its renters to
dictate to the rest of the audience.  There are six subsec-
tions shown.  If each bay contained twelve people (four
across and three deep), then the capacity of the entire gallery would have been seventy-two.  At three pence per
head (the standard price for such seats when De Witt was
in London) a packed gallery would have yielded the management 216d.  Reporting Henslowe's receipts, Alfred Harbage tells us that the maximum received for a performance
of an old play at the Rose theatre (comparable to the Swan
in size) was 1,728d (Harbage 1941: 28).[39]  Thus, Hotson's
influential spectators provided only one-eighth the revenue
of the playhouse.  Add a substantial number of stool-holders
and the percentage is still small.  It is clear that the spectators sitting behind the stage (if any) were not important
enough, economically speaking, to command the faces of
the actors.

Nor were they important enough as critics and taste-
makers.  The vast majority of surviving plays known to
have been written for the public playhouse are definitely
not designed to appeal primarily to the tastes of the gentry.
(This is not to say that the upper classes did not enjoy
them.)  If the plays had been written for a coterie audience,
they would be indistinguishable from plays first performed
in the private theatres.  This is obviously not the case.[40]

Finally, Hotson's reasoning from the practice of court
staging overlooks a basic difference between a royal hall
and a public theatre.  Plays at court were primarily
social and ceremonial occasions, made so by the presence
of the monarch.  The actors played to the Queen regardless
of how the hall was set up, and the courtiers were present
not to see the play so much as to see Elizabeth and if possible, be seen by her.  It is faulty reasoning to assume
that the four-fifths of the Globe audience who sat opposite
the gentry would have contented themselves with a glimpse

101

of the quality when they had paid as much as a full day's wages to see Richard Burbage. As for those gentry, we can guess from evidence elsewhere that even in the public theatres they were more eager to exhibit themselves than to see the play. The sight lines in most modern opera boxes are among the worst in the house, and the stage seats in the old Comédie Française showed the courtiers who sat on them little more that the back of Crébillon as he played Sémiramis. I see no reason to assume that the Elizabethan gulls and dandies would not have been content with as little.

Leslie Hotson's reconstruction of the Globe is unsound, but this fact should not prevent us from acknowledging and being grateful, not only for the wealth of fresh material he has unearthed, but for the sorely-needed jolt his arguments have given to our complacent beliefs in older theories that are not actually much better.

The previous sections have concentrated on the individual excellences and drawbacks of the various reconstructions under consideration. When we examine these conjectures as a group, we find, unfortunately, that their imperfections are considerably more prominent than their virtues. In the first place, every one of them, naturally, is based as far as possible on the surviving evidence, and we have seen again and again how poor this evidence is. Moreover, each reconstruction has been determined to a great extent by a particular theory of its creator. Since there are no adequate theories as yet, there are no accurate reconstructions. Finally, every scholar who has reconstructed a playhouse has selected details from the whole body of available evidence, often without any guide other than personal inclination. Presented, for example, with the huts shown in the De Witt, Visscher and Hollar drawings, each investigator has simply taken his pick.

When evaluating the work of a playhouse reconstructor we must keep these perennial drawbacks in mind and ask of each: what credentials do his sources carry, how has he selected evidence from them, and how reasonable and comprehensive is the theory guiding the selection? Then the final test is, how theatrical is the result? Despite the leavening of such professionals as Richard Southers and C. Walter Hodges, the ranks of the reconstructors have been recruited principally from the study. It is obvious, for stance, that John Cranford Adams is not completely familiar with the psychology of theatre and theatrical conventions and that Leslie Hotson has little or no idea of the inescapable physical limits imposed upon stage practice. A reconstruction that suffices as a theory is useless unless it also works as theatre.

A corollary of this fact is that the letter killeth. The more intricately detailed a reconstruction and the more dogmatically argued the assertions supporting these details, the less accurate and useful the reconstruction is likely to be. The approach which can best cope with the evidence, the various theories and the requirement of theatrical practicality is that which apprehends the spirit. A sketch by Hodges of a performance at the Hope is more truly informative than a dissertation by Cranford Adams on the hangings in the "study" because the former is a synthesis produced by a sound understanding of the facts filtered through a vivid and theatrically trained imagination.

Examined collectively, these reconstructions also indicate the most pressing problems facing historians of the theatre. First, the genealogy of the Elizabethan playhouse has not yet been made clear. Until all the ancestors mentioned here and there in this essay are sorted out and evaluated, their influence on the playhouse and particularly the tiring house cannot be determined. Settling the problems of the discovery space alone would constitute a greater single advancement than any made in the last half-century, but the question will not be disposed of until the pedigree of alcove, booth, mansion, or some combination of these has been indisputably established. Nor has there been enough systematic evaluation of the effect on the playhouses of changing styles in architecture and decoration.

The proponents of Tudor decoration base their arguments on the construction methods used on large wooden buildings, while those who advocate baroque décor point to contemporary fashion and note that the gaudily painted theatres must have kept up with the times. This debate is far from settled.

Certain purely practical problems of playhouse design are equally far from solution. Despite the careful work of Alfred Harbage and others on audience capacity, sitting and standing arrangements are still in doubt, and almost nothing is known about the division of the playhouse into the various areas determined by admission price. Closely allied to this is the problem of sight lines. Not only do we lack evidence concerning the picture the audience had of the stage, but also we have no indication of how much they expected to see. Finally, despite all the attention to the stages, tiring house, and special effects areas, no one has closely considered the more mundane appointments of the theatre: the dressing and storage rooms, the costume rooms, a small administrative area perhaps.

None of these questions can be answered until considerable attention has been paid to the methodology of reconstruction. The eclectic selection of evidence has already been deplored, and it follows that some systematic method of evaluation of sources must be developed. But there is a greater problem than this, and one that is very probably insoluble. Proceeding on the necessary but highly doubtful premise that people are logical, all the investigators with whom we have dealt have surveyed the evidence, noted the problems, and then sat down to invent the theatre which comes closest to solving them. Each has sought utility, flexibility, efficiency and beauty, and each reconstruction has been in some way a refinement of those that preceded it. Assuming for the moment that we know the purpose of the Elizabethan public stage, we shall one day come as close as the evidence permits to the playhouse which ideally serves that purpose. But the chances are very good that the Elizabethan playhouse was far from efficient. Its heritage was mixed, its development very rapid, and its numbers too few to have permitted much experimentation with and perfection of its many necessary features. William Burbage built the Theatre in 1576. Exactly where he looked for the components he used is not known, but it is certain that he had no single precedent on which to base his design. Between this date and the building of the First Globe only a very few playhouses were erected. In the almost four hundred years during which the modern Italianate stage has been developing, nobody has ever designed a particularly flexible and efficient playhouse, although literally hundreds of theatres have been built. It is hardly likely that in the three-odd decades between the building of the first and the last open playhouses a theatre more refined than any we possess today could have been designed.

Unfortunate though it be, scholars have no recourse but to continue to seek closer and closer joinings of form and function, despite the fact that the features on which they labor were most probably determined by non-reasonable influences of which they can have no conception. But if designing efficient theatres is less than satisfactory, designing calculatedly inefficient ones is absured. And so reconstructions of Elizabethan public playhouses must always be as far from accurate as the ideal is from the actual.

This is a rather unfortunate tone for the conclusion of this survey. It is only too easy to issue blanket condemnations of other work when one is in the unassailable position of never having hazarded a theory of one's own. Moreover, teachers, students and play-producers, all of whom need some idea of Shakespeare's stage, can hardly be expected to suspend judgment until such time as a completely sound reconstruction is developed. Which conjecture, then, is the soundest? In my opinion, Hodges' 1958 Globe is the most careful and conservative attempt yet made. This reconstruction combines a judicious selection of source materials with a thorough understanding of Elizabethan stage practice and a fine sense of theatricality.  Its defects, on the other hand, proceed more from the nature of the problem than from any theory of its creator.

# APPENDIX

## COMMONLY REPRODUCED
## MAPS AND VIEWS OF LONDON

In verifying the sources of reconstructions, the investigator is usually obliged to content himself with reproductions of the various maps and views most often cited as evidence for certain features of London public playhouses. These pictorial documents are apt to be confusing, not only because most of them have been assigned varying artists, titles, sources, and dates of execution and publication, but also because of frequent imperfections in the reproductions of them. The following list is not a catalogue of maps and views, but a brief attempt to list the most common of them, along with whatever information is known about their dates, artists, and relationships to other maps and views. Each document is listed by the name usually given it, and underlined maps and views are source documents, from which later, less authoritative versions have been derived. These derived maps and views are listed chronologically under their sources. Under each entry is a list of the more easily obtained books in which reproductions appear. An asterisk indicates a particularly useful reproduction and an X marks a reproduction that is unsuitable for some reason. As will be obvious from the list, Hodges 1953, Hubbard 1923, Shapiro 1948, and Smith 1956 are richest in material. All the books containing reproductions are listed in the bibliography.

1.   VAN DEN WYNGAERDE: view of London, Westminster, and Southwark ca. 1550.  Whole view (in three parts) in Besant 1904:  between 218-219, 234-235, 350-351.

2.   PART OF SOUTHWARK: anonymous map ca. 1550. Shapiro 1948:  Pl. V.

3.   HÖFNAGEL [ ?]: view of London published 1572 in Braun and Hogenberg's Civitas Orbis Terrarum, and often

referred to by the book title, or by those authors' names.
Various details in Q. Adams 1917: facing 31. 120: Q.
Adams 1923: facing 114; Braines 1921: 47; (*)Hubbard
1923: pl. 1; Smith 1956: pl. 1.

4.  AGAS: printed 1633; drawn between 1569-1590.
Bankside area probably based on Höfnagel. Various details in Q. Adams 1917: between 26-27, 123; Braines
1921: facing 52; (X)Hubbard 1923: pl. 2; Smith 1956: pl. 2.
Hubbard's reproduction contains modern overprinting.

5.  SMITH: view of the city, 1588, MS. complete view in
(*)Baker 1907: facing 18; Folger London. Detail in Q.
Adams 1917: facing 121. The Baker and Folger versions
are apparently different states of the view.

6.  NORDEN: 1593, printed in Speculum Britanniae.
Various details in C. Adams 1942: facing 18; Q. Adams
1917: 147; Q. Adams 1923: facing 126; Folger London;
(*)Hubbard 1923: pl. 3; (*)Shapiro 1948: pl. VI; Smith
1956: pl. 3.

7.  NORDEN: 1593-a. 2 states. Copied by Hondius as
inset in map of Middlesex published in Speed's Theatre of
the Empire of Great Britain. In Shakespeare Quarterly
vol. 9, 554.

8.  NORDEN: 1600. A revised version of the 1593 map,
inset in a view of London published in Civitas Londoni,
1600. Details in Halliday 1956: 81; (*)Hodges 1953: pl. 2;
Shapiro 1948: pl. VII; Smith 1956: pl. 4.

9.  CIVITAS LONDONI: 1600. View by Norden.
(*)Halliday 1956: 40-41; Hodges 1953: pl. 6; Shapiro 1948:
ppl. IV-b, VIII-a; (*)Smith 1956: pl. 5.

10. ABRAM BOOTH: View of London from the North, ca.
1600. Most of map in Halliday 1956: 28-29. Details in
Halliday 1956: 29; Hotson 1960: facing 308, 312.

11. DELERAM PORTRAIT: ca. 1610. Equestrian portrait of James I showing Bankside in background.

(X)C. Adams 1942: facing 18; (X)Q. Adams 1917: facing 246; (X)Folger Theatre; Shapiro 1948: pl. X; Smith 1956: pl. 6. The C. Adams, Q. Adams, and Folger versions are completely unreliable; they are reproductions of a 19th century mezzotint copy by Charles Turner. Turner has cut away part of a rise of ground to display more of one theatre than the original shows.

12. RYTHER [?] map. Unfinished version dated 1604; published between 1636-1645. Complete map in (*)Thorndike 1916: facing 38; Baker 1907: between 36-37. Various details in Q. Adams 1917: 278; Baker 1907: facing 125, 135.

13. RYTHER: finished version published between 1631-1656. Detail in Smith 1956: pl. 11.

14. HONDIUS: view of London inset in map of Great Britain and Ireland dated 1610 and published in Speed's History of the Theatre of Great Britain, 1611. Complete view in Q. Adams 1917: 149; Q. Adams 1923: facing 120; (X)Baker 1907: frontispiece; Hubbard 1923: pl. 11; (*)Shapiro 1948: pl. VIII-b; (X)Thorndike 1916: facing 32. Details in C. Adams 1942: facing 202; Smith 1956: pl. 7. The Baker and Thorndike reproductions are too faint to be of use. Whether they show another state of the original, a poor copy, or simply faulty reproduction is impossible to tell.

15. HOLLAND: 1620. Anonymous view derived from Hondius and published in Holland's Herⱷologica Anglica, 1620. Shapiro 1948: pl. 9-a.

16. BAKER: 1643. Anonymous view derived from Hondius and published as frontispiece of Baker's Chronicles, 1643. (*)Q. Adams 1917: 147; C. Adams 1942: 387.

17. VISSCHER: Panorama, 1616; British Museum copy. Complete view reproduced as a separate publication of the Folger Shakespeare Library. Various details in C. Adams 1942: facing 82; (X)Q. Adams 1917: 127, 165, 253;

(X)Q. Adams 1923: facing 266, 280; (X)Baker 1907: facing 165, 175; Braines 1921: facing 52; Folger Theatre; Halliday 1956: 82; Hodges 1953: pl. 1; Hubbard 1923: pl. 4; Smith 1956: pl. 9; Thorndike 1916: frontispiece. The reproductions in Q. Adams 1917, Q. Adams 1923, and Baker 1907 are all modern copies of the original.

18. VISSCHER: Folger Library copy, apparently an imperfect redrawing of the British Museum copy. Undated. Details in C. Adams 1942: frontispiece; Smith 1956: pl. 8.

19. MAP OF SOUTHWARK: 1620. Anonymous MS. In Smith 1956: pl. 16.

20. PORTRAIT OF JAMES I: 1621, anonymous equestrian portrait with Bankside in background. Shapiro 1948: pl. XI.

21. ANONYMOUS VIEW: 1621: a view copied from the background of the 1621 Portrait, with the details obscured in the source supplied from imagination. Shapiro 1948: pl. XII.

22. SURVEY OF PARIS GARDEN MANOR: ananymous map, 1627. Complete map in Q. Adams 1917: 163. Detail in Shapiro 1948: pl. IX-b.

23. INIGO JONES SKETCH: set-design sketch with small background showing Bankside, 1638. Complete sketch in Smith 1956: pl. 14; detail in Shapiro 1948: pl. XIV-a.

24. INIGO JONES SKETCH: another design with larger background, 1638. Complete sketch in Smith 1956: pl. 15. Detail in Shapiro 1948: pl. XIV-b.

25. MERIAN: view 1638, based partially on Visscher. Various details in Q. Adams 1917: facing 256; Braines 1921: 54; Folger Theatre; Hubbard 1923: pl. 5; Smith 1956: pl. 10.

26. HOWELL'S LONDINOPOLIS: view ascribed to Hollar, published in James Howell's Londinopolis, 1657. Derived from Merian. Baker 1907: facing 155; Thorndike 1916: 26; Hind 1922: pl. XXI.

27. LONDINUM URBS: probably early 18th century; a badly degenerate copy of Merian or Howell. Hubbard 1923: pl. 8; Hodges 1953: pl. 8.

28. HOLLAR SKETCH: a sketch of the bankside theatres and surroundings by Wenzel Hollar, 1644 or earlier. Hodges 1953: pl. 5; Shapiro 1949: ppl. XI, XII; Smith 1956: pl. 12.

29. HOLLAR VIEW: 1647 engraving of London, based on drawings including the Hollar sketch of 1644. Complete panorama (assembled and in separate plates) in Hind 1922: ppl. XV-XX, XX-a. Various details in C. Adams 1942: facing 138; Q. Adams 1917: facing 260, 326 (captions reversed); (X)Baker 1907: facing 165 (redrawn and called "The Rose?"); Braines 1921: 58; Halliday 1956: 111; Hodges 1953: pl. 4; Hubbard 1923: pl. 6; Shapiro 1948: pl. XIII; Smith 1956: pl. 13; Thorndike 1916: facing 222.

30. F. DEWIT: copied from Hollar between 1647-1660. Hubbard 1923: pl. 7.

31. FAITHORNE: 1658 map. Detail in Q. Adams 1917: 331.

32. HOLLAR POST FIRE: 1669 map. Complete map in Hind 1922: ppl. XII-XIII. Detail in Adams 1917: 331.

In addition to the above, the views of Wyck [?] before 1672, based on Merian; Moore 1662, copied from Hollar; and Porter ca. 1660 [?] are unimportant drawings excluded from this list because they have not been reproduced in any book. Many of the above documents, including these last three have been published full-size or only slightly reduced by the London Topographical Society. Unfortunately, these invaluable copies are sometimes difficult to get hold of.

## NOTES

1.  Perhaps the best brief summary of work on the Elizabethan stage as a whole is Wilson 1953. The better-known works of Lawrence and Reynolds are listed in the Bibliography.

2.  The most comprehensive attempts to evaluate these views are those of Smith (Smith 1956) and Shapiro (Shapiro 1948). See the critical list of reproductions following this article.

3.  See also the recently discovered engraving of a theatre which may be a drawing of an actual seventeenth century German theatre built, perhaps, for English actors. Bernheimer 1958.

4.  W. F. Rothwell is eloquent on this matter of differences (Rothwell 1959).

5.  Some of these views are reproduced in Hodges 1953: 128.

6.  Actually, says Hotson, it was Edward Capell who first suggested a rear stage, in 1774. Malone's supplement to the Johnson and Steevens Shakespeare was not published until 6 years later (Hotson 1960: 100-101).

7.  It should be understood that, in this article, the term "baroque" is used in its most general sense: not as the label of a particular architectural style, but as the description of an approach to decorating characterized by capricious, convoluted ornaments and encrustations, "... an architecture cut, as it were, out of parchment or leather, a light-as-air architecture writhing and curvetting in space," (Summerson 1953: 24).

8.  In most of my proportional calculations I have used dividers to measure a human figure (calling it six feet) and then compared this measurement with features at the same "depth" in the drawing. An alternate method is to assume that the artist has employed the gallery heights

specified by the Fortune contract (twelve, eleven and nine feet) and then derive the scale from a proportion based on the heights of these galleries in the actual drawing.

9. After this reconstruction had been published a picture of the Curtain was found in a view of London, looking down the Thames rather than across it. See Hotson 1960: Appendix B.

10. The Fortune and Hope contracts have been reproduced in many works, among them, Chambers 1923, C. Adams 1942, Hodges 1953, and Smith 1956.

11. Described in Nagler 1958: 26-28. A drawing of Tieck's model was made and published by Hodges (Hodges 1959: 12).

12. An interesting variation on Tieck's reconstruction is the subject of a notice by Förster (Förster 1916). In 1836, Wolf Grafen von Baudissin published a collection of his translations of Elizabethan plays: Ben Jonson und seine Schule, dargestellt in einer Auswahl von Lustspielen und Tragödien, übersetzt und erläutert durch Wolf Grafen von Baudissin. Leipzig, 1836. He included a reconstruction by Gottfried Semper, an associate of Tieck's at Dresden. According to von Baudissin, Semper's reconstruction, a modification of Tieck's, was submitted to Tieck, who endorsed it after suggesting a few further alterations. The reconstruction, reproduced in Förster 1916, is very similar to Hodges' sketch of Tieck's model (Hodges 1959: 12). An illustration by Hauschild in the same article is an interesting, if fanciful attempt at a "typical" theatre.

13. Reproductions showing these theatres can be found in Hodges 1953: 156-157.

14. The calculation is based on Hodges' forty-five-foot yard plus the combined depths of the Fortune galleries. A five-foot deviation either way in the case of the Second Globe would not invalidate my argument.

15. Proof of the impracticality of this system is furnished

by a picture of the "Elizabethan stage" used at Harvard by George Pierce Baker (Baker 1907: facing 250). This photograph shows the unlucky gallery sitters craning to see around the closed curtains. William Poel's famous stage was similar. Both stages used the side curtains but not the side walls. For interior scenes, all three curtains were drawn.

16. George R. Kernodle suggests a similar arrangement. See below.

17. It was Albright who showed that the drawing from The Wits does not represent the Red Bull playhouse.

18. Corbin's reconstruction, as drawn by George Varian (plate six-bottom) was apparently the unacknowledged source of an often-reproduced drawing made under the direction of S.A. Tannenbaum and published in Oliphant 1929. Aside from a few trivial additions and subtractions: stage railings, details of the back wall of the inner stage, traps and flying openings etc., the second drawing is clearly a copy of the first. The only notable additions are two second level window stages and windows beside the tiring house doors. The later drawing has also been published on the inside back cover of the Shakespeare Association Bulletin IV (January, 1929), and as the frontispiece of Lawrence 1935. A model designed by G.W. Small and reproduced in Small 1935, is based roughly on the copy of Corbin's reconstruction.

19. It is not really fair to patronize Corbin. The storm scenes in most productions are still cluttered with flashing spotlights and tin thunder.

20. A lucid and well-illustrated account of Renaissance English architecture can be found in Summerson 1953, to which this paragraph owes much of its substance. Blomfield 1897, another standard work on the subject, is criticized by Summerson for being over-concerned with proving a theory of architectural development and decay.

21. Hodges has acknowledged his indebtedness of Kernodle.

22. Hodges' theory is depicted graphically by a series of drawings showing the development of the pavilion (Hodges 1953: 170-173). Hodges does not claim to have invented the pavilion, but notes that Chambers came to "a very tentative thought about it." (letter to the present writer.)

23. The phrase in question, for which see Platter 1929: 37, is "... hiezwischen stige der engellender in die Zelten..." Schanzer 1956 is devoted to comments on the translation of Platter's passage about the theatre, but Professor Nagler considers these glosses open to question.

24. Interesting light on the controversy between proponents of "inner" and "pavilion" discovery spaces is cast by an article of Charles Tyler Prouty's (Prouty 1953). Professor Prouty discovered records indicating that between 1557 and 1568, plays were very frequently performed in Trinity Hall, a building connected with St. Botolph's Church in London. Detailed architectural sketches made in the late eighteenth century give us a complete picture of the hall, the gallery of which particularly concerns us here. In most Tudor halls the space between this gallery (running along the end of the room behind which are the pantry, buttery, and so-forth) is concealed by a screen; in Trinity Hall it was open, and provided with a door in back opening onto a vestry, and another in one side wall, behind which was a spiral staircase. The staircase, in turn, ended at a door onto the gallery itself. Curtains hung from the front edge of the gallery floor would have provided a perfect discovery space below, complete with three entrances (between and around each side of the two curtains) and a concealed approach to the gallery above. The trouble is that this evidence can be taken in either of two ways. If the end wall of the hall is considered to be the "tiring house wall" then the gallery arrangement is clearly a proto-pavilion built out from the "tiring house." But since the spaces above and below the gallery floor are open only on their front side, they very closely

resemble an "inner stage." Since Prouty's article is descriptive and historical, it does not examine these possibilities. In any event, Trinty Hall is of enormous importance to us, because it is, to my knowledge, the only building regularly used by Elizabethan professional actors that we can reconstruct with any degree of confidence.

25. This reconstruction has been widely reproduced. A large and beautiful model is on loan to the Folger Library, and at least one full size stage has been based on it. The plates reproduced are Irwin Smith's detailed scale drawings. A few discrepencies between the dimensions shown and those of Adams' original theory will be found, because Smith corrected some of Adams' errors.

26. A photograph of a model based on Cranford Adams' early reconstruction was published in Folger Theatre 1935. After the building of the model based on the second reconstruction, a picture of this second model silently replaced the earlier photo. The pictures can easily be told apart since the first reconstruction has a rectangular stage.

27. Imagine The Alchemist, almost all of which takes place inside Lovewit's house, staged according to Adams' theory.

28. Significantly, Adams praises the Norden 1593 map, but does not mention the revised version of 1600, on which the newly built Globe appears as a round building (C. Adams 1942: 385).

29. The briefest comparison of the Hollar and Visscher panoramas, both reproduced full-size by the London Topographical Society, makes this opinion seem strange indeed.

30. Adams' ground plan shows the true dimensions of forty-one and eighty-three feet (C. Adams 1942: 53). It is indeed possible to derive a forty-three foot stage: if you contradict the Fortune contract and call the gallery depth twelve and one half feet plus wall, or thirteen feet,

116

then the modular unit is twelve and one half feet rather than twelve, the Globe sections become twenty-five feet across the inner face, the yard becomes sixty-one feet wide, and the building becomes eighty-four feet wide, the figure Adams gives. A stage placed according to Adams' specifications in this larger theatre is exactly forty-three feet wide. Of course, disregarding the Fortune specifications invalidates the argument anyway. Smith has noted this discrepency (I. Smith 1956: 32n). It should also be noted that Adams subsequently realized his mistake, as a passing reference to the stage dimensions in a later article shows (C. Adams 1948: 315).

31. This delightful book, meant primarily for children, is nonetheless an important work of scholarship.

32. Unfortunately, I was unable to obtain a copy of this drawing in time to reproduce it here. Because it is unquestionably the best reconstruction yet made, and because it is not a book illustration but a large print on heavy paper (app. twenty-two by thirty inches) this drawing should be especially useful to teachers of Shakespeare and Elizabethan drama. The print is obtainable from Coward-McCann Inc. in New York or Ernest Benn Ltd. in London. This reconstruction, or one very similar to it was the source of a model made by Hodges and Southern for an Encyclopaedia Britannica film on Shakespeare, and now on display at the Shakespeare Festival Theatre, Stratford, Connecticut.

33. Professor Nicoll would supply such doors for action proceeding from the yard to the stage and back again (Nicoll 1959).

34. We shall confine our discussion to Hotson 1960, since Hotson 1953 is an introductory article and Hotson 1954 is devoted primarily to "private" performances.

35. For pictorial material, see Hodges 1953 and Kernodle 1944.

36. E.g. his "dismissal" of Nagler; Hotson 1960:  164.

37. Dr. Hotson has considered the problem of light in the tiring house.  In a letter to Mr. John Worthen (later quoted in a letter from Dr. Hotson to me) he says,

> "Possibly the set railings before the tiring-house windows to hold off the spectators; or more probably they sloped the ground down sharply, starting three or four feet from the edge of the stage.  Such an operation would answer three purposes:  (1) Keep people back, giving light, (2) Form a drain to lead off the water from the yard, and (3) provide the excavation to give the additional head-room desirable in the tiring-house."

(Italics Hotson's.)  Again, we are excavating the Bankside marsh.

38. Again, no interior view shows any trace of such scaffolding.  Even if the De Witt view showed a rehearsal, as Professor Nagler has suggested, these "houses" would have been necessary.  But, says Hotson (in the letter cited in note thirty-seven, above), "There is no evidence that the artist of the Swan drawing was intent on recording the details of an unfamiliar theatre.  On the contrary, according to his own account (see Chambers) his purpose was no more than to point out certain 'Roman' or circus features of the English amphiteatra (e.g., the amphitheattrical arrangement, with the excellent seats—like the emperor's podium—close up on the protected side of the ring, the cover over the stage—similar to the Roman velum—, the orchestra, sedilia, porticus, arena: all Roman)." (Italics Hotson's.)  He goes on to note that the artist of the De Witt drawing also left out the hangings and posts called for in the contracts because they were medieval, rather than Roman features.  If Hotson's explanation is true, it would be interesting to know how De Witt could see the parts of the playhouse concealed behind Hotson's scaffolding, and why the orchestra was "close

up on" the protected area rather than actually under heavens, where Hotson's most distinguished guests sat.

39.  The figure is for October 1, 1594.  It might be objected
that we are far from certain as to what receipts Henslowe
received.  Perhaps the figures used by Harbage do not
represent total admissions, but only Henslowe's share.
However, Harbage has provided a cross-check by com-
puting the number of spectators that could have been ac-
commodated in a theatre of the Fortune's dimensions.

40.  Harbage 1941, Chapter Three, and Harding 1954 show
in some detail that the most numerous and influential
group of play-goers belonged to what a modern sociologist
might call the lower-middle and middle-middle classes.

# PLATES

# ACKNOWLEDGEMENTS and LIST OF PLATES

PLATE ONE (Top): The reconstruction of William Archer and Walter H. Godfrey. First appeared in The London Tribune, October 12, 1907. Elevation. (Bottom): The Archer-Godfrey reconstruction. View. Both from A Companion to Shakespeare Studies, Harley Granville-Barker and G. B. Harrison, eds. Cambridge University, 1934.

PLATE TWO (Left): The Archer-Godfrey reconstruction. Plan. From A Companion to Shakespeare Studies, Harley Granville-Barker and G. B. Harrison, eds. Cambridge University Press, 1934. (Right): The reconstruction of Cecil Brodmeier, reproduced from Brodmeier, 1904. Plan.

PLATE THREE (Left): The Albright reconstruction. View. From The Shakespearian Stage, by Victor E. Albright. Columbia University Press, 1909. (Right): The Halliday reconstruction. View. From Shakespeare: a Pictorial Biography by F. E. Halliday. Studio Books, New York.

PLATE FOUR (Top): The Nicoll reconstruction. View. From The Development of the Theatre by Allardyce Nicoll. George G. Harrap and Company Ltd. 1927. (Bottom): The Kernodle reconstruction. View. From From Art to Theatre by George R. Kernodle. University of Chicago Press. Copyright 1944 by the University of Chicago.

PLATE FIVE (Left): The reconstruction of G. Topham Forrest, from Forest 1921. Plan. (Right): Forrest's reconstruction. Elevation. Both from The Site of the Globe Playhouse by W. W. Braines. London County Council, 1921. Reproduced by permission of the London County Council.

PLATE SIX (Top): The Q. Adams reconstruction. View. From A Life of William Shakespeare by Joseph Quincy Adams. Houghton Mifflin Company, 1923. Drawing by Henry Roenne. (Bottom): The reconstruction of John Corbin, from Corbin 1911. View.

PLATE SEVEN: A Hodges reconstruction. View. From Shakespeare and the Players by C. Walter Hodges. Coward-McCann, Inc., 1948. Used by permission of Coward-McCann, Inc., publishers.

PLATE EIGHT: The Hotson reconstruction. View. From Shakespeare's Wooden O by Leslie Hotson. Rupert Hart-Davis, Ltd., 1960.

PLATE NINE: Hotson's reconstruction. Detail showing the actor's progress from the tiring house below the stage to the second level of a "mansion." From Shakespeare's Wooden O by Leslie Hotson. Rupert Hart-Davis, ltd., 1960.

PLATE TEN: The reconstruction of John Cranford Adams, first published in 1942. These drawings are by Irwin Smith, and appear in I. Smith 1956. Diagram showing principal dimensions. (The small plan of the Globe in the upper corner indicates the angle of view.) Reproduced with the permission of Charles Scribners' Sons from Shakespear's Globe Playhouse by Irwin Smith. Copyright© 1956 Charles Scribners' Sons. Plates eleven and twelve are from the same source.

PLATE ELEVEN: Cranford Adams' reconstruction. Section.

PLATE TWELVE: Cranford Adams' reconstruction. Plan.

NOTE: Considerations of space and difficulties in obtaining reproduction rights have made it impossible to reprint some reconstructions. In addition to these, drawings appearing in Chambers 1923, Hodges 1953, and the various numbers of the annual Shakespeare Survey have been omitted on the assumption that investigators interested in reconstructions will have these important publications at hand.

Too late for inclusion here, I discovered a fine reconstruction by Richard Leacroft in his The Theatre, London, 1958.

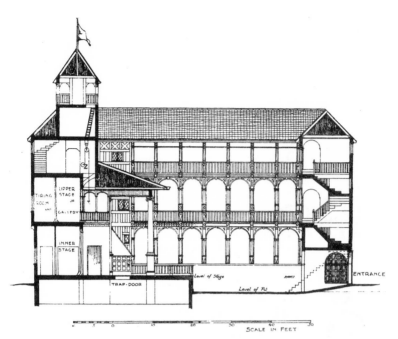

Elevation.   Archer — Godfrey Reconstruction

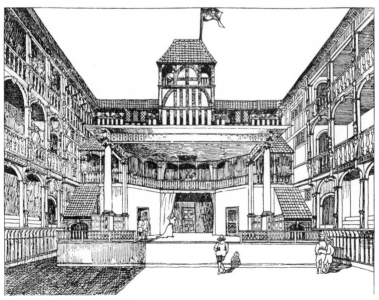

View.   Archer — Godfrey Reconstruction

PLATE ONE

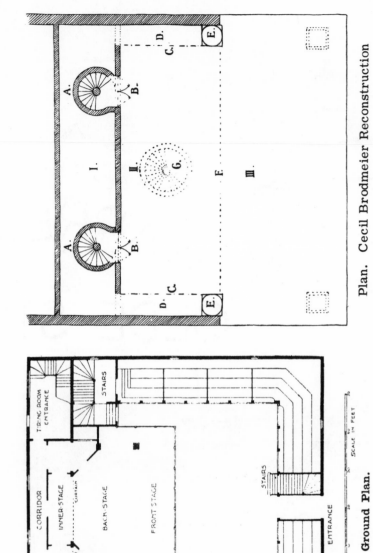

Plan. Cecil Brodmeier Reconstruction

Ground Plan.

SCALE IN FEET

PLATE TWO

View.   Albright Reconstruction

PLATE THREE

From Shakespeare: a Pictorial Biography
by F. E. Halliday.  Studio Books, New York

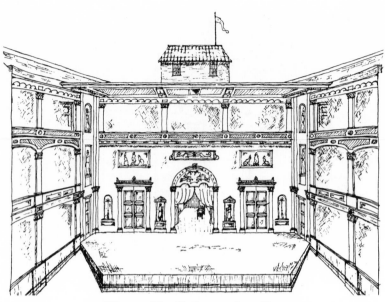

View. Nicoll Reconstruction

View. Kernodle Reconstruction

PLATE FOUR

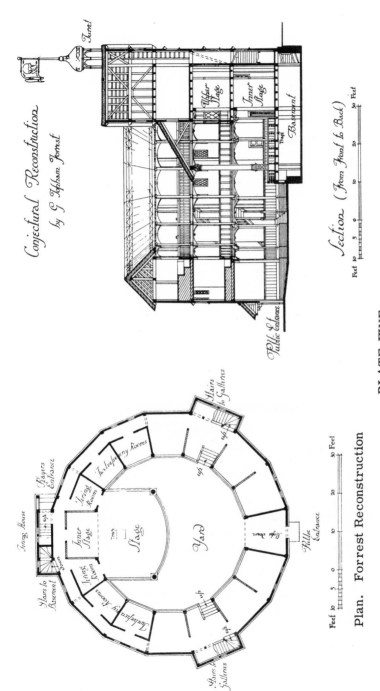

Conjectural Reconstruction
by G. Topham Forrest

Section (from Front to Back)

Turret

Upper Stage

Inner Stage

Basement

Trap

Publ. & Public Entrance

Feet 10 5 0 10 20 30 Feet

Tiring House

Players Entrance

Stairs to Basement

Tiring Room

Inner Stage

The Stage

Tiring Rooms

Twopenny Rooms

Threepenny Rooms

Stairs to Galleries

Yard

Light down

Public Entrance

Stairs to Galleries

Feet 10 5 0 10 20 30 Feet

Plan. Forrest Reconstruction

PLATE FIVE

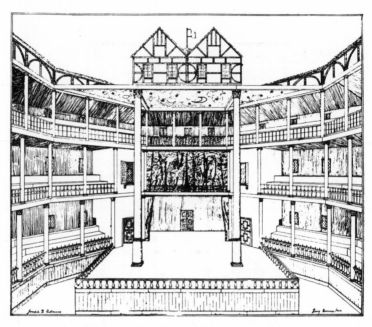

View.  Q. Adams Reconstruction

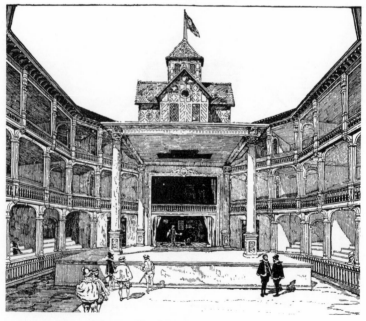

View.  Corbin Reconstruction

PLATE SIX

THE
GLOBE PLAYHOUSE
1599–1613
A Conjectural Reconstruction
by
C. Walter Hodges

KEY

A. The "Hut", with machinery for lowering the "Heavenly" throne to the stage.
B. The "Heavens".
C. Top stage, sometimes used as a music gallery.
D. Upper stage.
E. Window stages.
F. Inner stage, sometimes called the "Study".
G. Trap, leading down to the "Hell" under the stage.
H. "Gentlemen's Rooms" or "Lords Rooms".
J. Storage lofts, dressing rooms, etc.
K. Dressing rooms.
L. Backstage area.
M. Main entrances to auditorium.
N. Doorways connecting with gallery staircase.
O. Entrance to galleries and staircases.

Gallery
Staircases

PLATE SEVEN

View.   Hotson Reconstruction

PLATE EIGHT

Detail. Hotson Reconstruction

PLATE NINE

DRAWING XV

THE PRINCIPAL DIMENSIONS
OF THE GLOBE PLAYHOUSE

*as reconstructed by*
*John Cranford Adams*

Music Gallery 11' 6"

22' 6" between centers of Stage Posts

Aperture of Chamber 21' 6"

Over all width of Playhouse 84' 6"

Aperture of Alcove 23' 0"

Width of Yard 55' 0"

Width at rear of Platform 41' 6"

Width at front of Platform 24' 0"

10' overhang

12' 6"

21' 6"

PLATE TEN

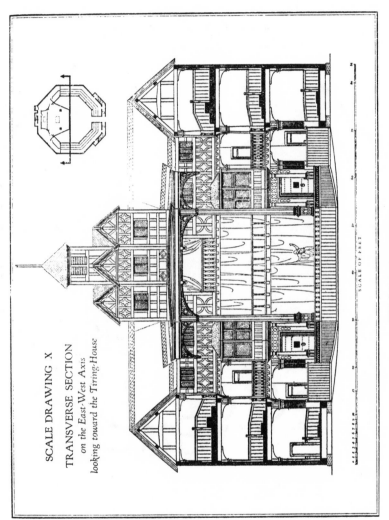

SCALE DRAWING X

TRANSVERSE SECTION
on the *East-West Axis*
*looking toward the Tiring-House*

SCALE OF FEET

PLATE ELEVEN

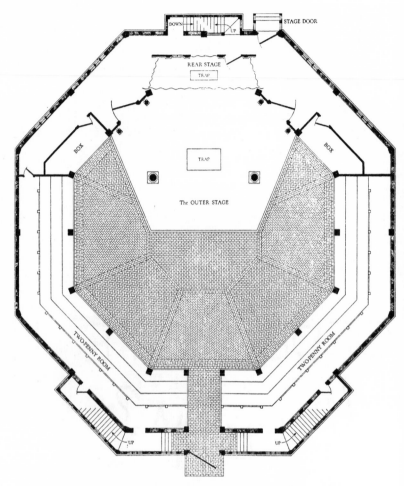

Plan.   C. Adams Reconstruction

PLATE TWELVE

# DEVELOPMENT AND OPERATION OF
# THE FIRST BLACKFRIARS THEATRE


by

Robert K. Sarlos

# INTRODUCTION

"But in playes either those things are fained that never were, as Cupid and Psyche plaid at Paules; and a great many Cōmedies more at y$^e$ Black friers and in every Playe House in London, which for breuities sake I ouer skippe." (Gosson 1582: 188).

Stephen Gosson's sentence shows as well as any, in what darkness we proceed when studying the Elizabethan period. The virtue of "breuitie" will be our constant curse. compelling chroniclers to "ouer skippe" information that is of the greatest importance to us.

The Blackfriars, of course, has long been known as the home of two successive playhouses. The second of these, established by Burbage in 1596, had great success with a company called the Children of Blackfriars. Because of Shakespeare's share in it, this enterprise has received considerable attention. Of the First Blackfriars Theatre, however, little was known before this century. Aside from Gosson's quotation, only one indication of this early enterprise was known: the plays of John Lyly Campaspe and Sapho and Phao, both printed in 1584, contain prologues "at the Black Fryers" placed in the text before the prologue at Court, a fact suggesting that they were played at both places before publication. (Lyly 1902: vol. 2; 313, 336). The key to real knowledge about the first Blackfriars Theatre was buried in the Revels Accounts, and was unearthed early in this century by Professor Albert Feuillerat (Documents 1908). These documents contain references to plays performed at Court by the Children of Windsor, and mention the name of their master, Richard Farrant, in connection with the Blackfriars. Only since the discovery in the Loseley MSS of leases and various letters pertaining to the history of the whole theatrical enterprise during the years 1576-1585, has the picture become somewhat clearer.[1] Shortly before and after 1910, Professor Feuillerat published several articles pointing towards a flourishing enterprise at the Blackfriars, and almost simultaneously Professor Charles W. Wallace wrote a history of this theatre based in part on the documents discovered by Feuillerat (Feuillerat 1910-a; Feuillerat 1912; Wallace 1912).[2] Apart from these studies, the most important works on the subject are those of Hillebrand and Brawner (Hillebrand 1926; Brawner 1942). In addition, Alfred Harbage presents a terse summary (Harbage 1952).

The purpose of this paper is to summarize all that we know about the First Blackfriars Theatre. I shall begin with a survey of the theatrical background, then discuss in detail the events immediately preceding and leading up to the establishment of the First Blackfriars Theatre and shed some light on its operation. An attempt will be made to bring the most crucial issues into focus, and to suggest possible further research to supplement our present picture.

The significance of a study of the First Blackfriars Theatre lies in the fact that through it we may hope to increase our knowledge about (a) the rôle of the boys' companies and their situation, (b) the origins, distinguishing features, and operation of the "private" playhouses, (c) John Lyly's growth into a playwright of stature, and (d) the turning point that occurred with the emergence after 1586, of such playwrights as Marlowe, Lodge, Greene, Peele, and finally Shakespeare.

# I. DEVELOPMENT AND DECLINE OF THE FIRST BLACKFRIARS THEATRE

## Theatrical Background

The third quarter of the sixteenth century witnessed a remarkable increase in theatrical activity. While the local guilds persisted in the presentation of mystery cycles, and the universities were laboring to revive the classical theatre by producing the plays of Seneca, Terence, and their numerous imitators, two other forms of playacting sprang into full bloom: the strolling players invaded London — some settling permanently in the city — and the child actors began gaining in popularity. The child actors (some of whom became the actors of the First Blackfriars Theatre) were originally and primarily choirboys. There had been a chapel attached to the Royal Household since the days of Henry I, the function of which was to celebrate divine service. In the time of Edward IV it was composed of 24 gentlemen and 8 children. Later on there were usually 12 children, while the number of gentlemen fluctuated. Perhaps in the earliest times the chapel had strictly adhered to its primary function, but by the early part of the twelfth century the gentlemen were participating in entertainment other than choral singing; and it gradually became customary for the group of choirboys to appear with them in pageants and masques (Hillebrand 1926: 40-41). There are six references before 1500 (the first of them from the early twelfth century) indicating that children took part in plays performed at Court, although, except for the one in 1487 at the Court of Henry VII they are all rather vague (Hillebrand 1926: 9-11). Thus the most important group of child actors, and that with the longest history, "The Children of the Chapel Royal" took shape. Under the leadership of the Master of the Children (first simply their schoolmaster), who was responsible for training the choirboys, they received an increasing share in the pageants. Later on, the master became the author as well as the director of the entertainment. It was finally William

141

Cornish, master from 1509 to 1523, who set the Children of the Chapel to playacting as a regular activity (Hillebrand 1926: 51).

Christmas 1515 can well be called a milestone in the development, not only of the child actors, but of English theatre and dramatic literature as well. For then, for the first time, the Chapel children took a prominent place as actors presenting the interlude of Troilus and Pandar (ibid. 55). We know that in the fall of 1519 the company consisted of seven children and that by this time Cornish was certainly the author of the plays presented (ibid. 57). Therefore, Wallace is correct in ranking Cornish as the first promoter of theatre arts and the father of English actor-managers. But it is going rather far to call him the founder of English drama (Wallace 1912: 37, 59). As we don't have any of his plays, we do not know what influence he had on writers who followed him.

Under the mastership of Richard Bower, 1545-1561, the first outlines of the theatre season appeared, and the Christmas presentation of plays by the Children of the Chapel became customary. The next master, Richard Edwards, was the first to leave us a play. It is Damon and Pythias, and is steeped in classical tradition. The abundant moral lessons and proverbs are what we might expect from a schoolmaster-turned-playwright. The succession in 1567 of William Hunnis to the mastership marks the beginning of the time that is of special interest to us. We know that the plays performed remained in the classical tradition, that the children played on Sundays, and that the Queen's Chapel served as their theatre (Hillebrand 1926: 86). This, then is the time, early in the reign of Elizabeth, that the child actors began to flourish. Beside the Children of the Chapel, the Children of St. Paul's (a choirboys' group dating back to at least 1312) now assumed greater importance under the mastership of Sebastian Westcote, ?1551-1582. Ten in number, they began producing plays at Court and established a theatre, probably in the house of the almoner and choirmaster (ibid. 114).

The third company, the one most closely connected with
the birth of the Blackfriars Theatre, had just been formed
at this time: the Children of Windsor.

Before turning to this group, to their master, Richard
Farrant, and to the immediate circumstances of the establishing of their theatre in the precinct of Blackfriars, let
us look at the general theatrical situation. There was
such an abundance of strolling actors' companies in the
city (who furnished part of the Court entertainment) that
in 1572 a "restrictive statute" was passed, legalizing only
companies under noble patronage. Legalization meant a
chance to appear before the Queen and the right to present
plays to the public without persecution. Therefore the
statute was followed by a strong striving for permanency.
The companies that obtained patronage also secured permanent headquarters where they could practice regularly.
As this was carried on with an audience present, it meant
not only the improvement of the performance to be presented at Court, but also additional income. Thus it is
that the companies settled at the Bull, the Bell Savage,
the Cross Keys and other inns. The more firmly settled
they became, however, the less did the city authorities
like them. One can judge the extent of theatrical activity
by the number of regulations and furious pamphlets directed
against the theatres. But every worthwhile enterprise
doubles its energy when it encounters obstacles. This
happened to the acting companies too. Their popularity
and therefore their activity increased rapidly, not only in
their theatres, but also at Court. From the year 1572 on
there was no Christmas without playacting before Elizabeth
(Chambers 1923: vol. 4; 88ff). The season that lasted
regularly from Christmas day to Twelfth Night, extended
from 1573 on (more often than not to include Shrovetide),
and gave opportunity for a good number of companies to
appear. Still, with the great expansion of theatrical activity and the increase in the number of acting groups, the
competition became rather tough on the child actors. The
adult companies had a distinct advantage over them:

permanent theatres, where audiences provided them with
both a chance to practice and an income.

## Development under Richard Farrant

Richard Farrant is known to have been a gentleman of
the Chapel Royal by 1553 (Chambers 1923: vol. 2; 36).  He
was a noteworthy composer of both services and songs.
Sometime before 1561 he married Annis, daughter of
Richard Bower, Master of the Children of the Chapel
(Hillebrand 1926:  65).  Farrant must have known (and
probably liked) the work his father-in-law was pursuing,
and might even have aspired to succeed him at the time
of the latter's death in 1561, for three years later, on
April 24, 1564, Farrant resigned from the Chapel to become organist and master of the choristers at St. George
Chapel, Windsor, in which capacity he received an annual
sum £81 6s 8d, plus lodging (DNB Farrant).[3]  Three years
later at Shrovetide (Feb. 9-11), his Children of Windsor
presented their first play before the Queen, for which
Farrant received £6 13s 4d, a sum he was to receive each
time he presented a play.  I think it safe to assume that
Farrant started to train his choristers for playacting as
soon as he became their master.  Considerable time for
preparation would have been necessary, since neither the
boys nor their master had done this kind of work before.
Moreover, they might not have been chosen to play before
the Queen during the first year of their existence.  The
authority of the Master of the Revels to "audition" the
groups, to see their whole repertoires, and then to choose
suitable plays strongly suggests this.  But Farrant undoubtedly did a good job of training, for from then on, in
each of the next ten seasons he presented his Children of
Windsor at Court in a play.[4]

New Year's day 1572 is an important date, for it gives
us the first title.  That day, we learn, the Children of
Windsor, under the leadership of Richard Farrant presented Ajax and Ulysses.  Though we do not have the play,
the title alone shows that Farrant, in accordance with the

144

practice established by the masters of the Children of the
Chapel, proceeded in the classical tradition. The next
play, the title of which is unknown, was presented on New
Year's Day 1573. (Chambers 1923: vol. 4; 88). Then followed Quintus Fabius on January 6, 1574; Xerxes on January 6, 1575, and "a playe" on St. John's Day (Dec. 27),
1575.[5] Then we mark another turn with the presentation
of Mutius Scaevola by the combined forces of the Children
of Windsor and the Chapel, on January 6, 1577. As the
short career of the Children of Windsor as a playacting
group came abruptly and mysteriously to a stop with this
performance, and as Richard Farrant appeared from then
on as the Master of the Children of the Chapel, we will re-
trace our steps a few months to look at the events leading
to this turning point.

In 1576, after ten years of successful play-producing
with the Children of Windsor, Farrant leased six rooms in
the Blackfriars precinct, an enclave within the walls of
London, but not under city jurisdiction. The buildings of
the old priory were not strange to him; the Office of Revels
had formerly been there. He asked his friend, Sir Henry
Neville, a former lessee of the premises, to commend
him to the owner, Sir William Moore, and they both wrote
to Moore on August 27. He granted their request, as well
as a second one concerning an additional room and the
tearing down of one partition; and the lease was drawn up.[6]
From later legal proceedings that will be discussed below,
we know that Farrant pulled down more than the permitted
one partition, "spoiled the windows," said Moore, and used
the premises for "a continuall howse for plays".[7]

Let us probe into Farrant's reasons for acting as he
did. It should be remembered that the Children lacked
continual practice in front of an audience as well as financial support, while the public companies enjoyed both.
Farrant, no doubt, wanted the regular practice which
would polish the performance of his troupe and thus win
them more frequent appearances at Court, not to mention
the additional income to be derived from public "rehearsals."

As the Children were, in effect, the property of the Crown, he could not openly admit this second purpose. Therefore Farrant pretended to Moore that he was only using the house for a school. In these circumstances the Children's company would probably not have made use of publicity as the adult companies did: no flags would have been raised, no bills posted. This and the size of playhouse available (depending, to a large extent on the master's ability to pay rent) would have limited the size of the audience, and proportionately higher admission would have been charged. All this meant that Farrant had to find an audience refined of taste and fat of purse; he had to locate his theatre in a fashionable neighborhood, where he would not be subject to the regulations of the city authorities. I therefore agree wholeheartedly with W. J. Lawrence's conclusion that the Blackfriars was a theatre of the courtier class (Lawrence 1921). The Blackfriars, as Feuillerat remarks, was just the place Farrant needed: an old monastery consisting of conveniently arranged buildings, in an aristocratic and well-frequented section of London that was convenient to the heavily travelled Thames, yet not within the jurisdiction of the city (Feuillerat 1910-a: 270; Adams 1917b: 15). To this we might add that the moment for opening was just as fitting as the place: Richard Farrant suddenly had two children's groups on his hands (discussed below, pp. 148ff). This explanation, however, does not satisfy Hillebrand. He thinks the want of better rehearsal hall "too slight motive for so radical a step," forgetting the most important difference between the Chapel and the new lodgings: in the former a paying audience was not permitted (Hillebrand 1926: 96). Instead he calls attention to the fact that after 1584, when they were deprived of their lease at Blackfriars, they ceased to play altogether until 1600, at which time they began again under a new master and in a new theatre (ibid. 97). Hillebrand concludes, therefore, that in 1567 the Children were barred from the use of the Chapel forever, and this is why they moved to Blackfriars. I propose that the reason they were deprived of the Chapel as

a place for rehearsal was the inadmissibility there of an
audience, which would be a source of inspiration to the
actors and money to their master.  The whole move is, in
fact, a step toward professionalism.  While the Children
continued to participate regularly in royal church services
as choirboys, they had so far appeared only once a year at
Court as actors.  Now it is virtually impossible to keep a
group of actors rehearsing for years without giving a performance, and to build up a repertoire the bulk of which
will never be performed.  If one is bent on maintaining a
theatre troupe—and from the pains the masters took it is
obvious that they were bent on it—there is no choice but
to secure an audience that will provide both creative and
financial stimulus.  As this step of Farrant's company
towards professionalism was not quite in line with custom,
it had to be taken rather inconspicuously.

Once Farrant had rented the rooms he would doubtless
have put them to use without delay.  On the basis of similar
cases, Wallace suggests that though the lease was only
signed on December 20, the Children occupied the premises
in time to rehearse for the season.  It will be remembered
that the two companies presented their combined production
of Mutius Scaevola on following Twelfth Night, January 6,
1577.  The lease then, valid from September 29, would
have permitted a three-month rehearsal period.[8]  Feuillerat, however, considers it probable that the first performance in the new theatre did not take place until the
end of 1577, since after their combined performance of
Twelfth Night, 1577, the Children of the Chapel did not appear at Court again until December 27, 1578, and Farrant
could have justified using the theatre for rehearsals much
earlier (Feuillerat 1910-a:  271-272; Feuillerat 1912:  85).[9]

It is clear from the records that Richard Farrant continued to present his Children in a play at Court every year
until his death.  On St. John's day (December 27) 1577, he
presented "a playe," and the following year on the same
day, The Historie of ...  This performance must have
been very successful, for at the end of the season, Shrove

Monday (March 2) 1579 he presented another play, The Historie of Loyaltie and beautie which, judging from its title, is the first play to break away from the classical tradition, and probably a romance. The next season, the last one Farrant was to participate in, he produced The Historie of Alucius, on St. John's day 1579. Sometime during the course of 1580 he was paid "pro commedia" at Lincoln's Inn, a fact that certainly counted as an honor (earlier, Richard Edwards had been acknowledged in the same way) (Chambers 1923: vol. 2; 36). This production at Lincoln's Inn must have been Farrant's last, for he died in November of the same year.[10]

It is puzzling that the plays presented by Farrant, between the acquisition of the rooms at Blackfriars and his death, are credited to the Children of the Chapel, with the exception of Mutius Scaevola, performed in cooperation with the Children of Windsor, who after this disappear as actors forever (Wallace 1912: 206-207). Farrant, of course, had strong ties with the Chapel, and in 1569 (five years after his resignation in order to assume the mastership at Windsor) was reinstated there as a gentleman. But the Master of the Children of the Chapel had been, since 1567 (the year, incidentally, of the first performance by the Windsor Children), William Hunnis, and there is no explanation for his replacement by Farrant, the master of the Windsor Company. We know that Hunnis was in good health, and that he had a large share in the Kenilworth festivities in 1575 (Stopes n. d.). Nor was he out of favor, for after Farrant's death he immediately took over the Children, as well as the theatre at Blackfriars.[11]

Chambers discusses Farrant's replacement of Hunnis as "part of a somewhat considerable theatrical enterprise," and declares it to be "pretty clear, that, although Farrant is described as Master of the Chapel's Children by the Treasurer of the Chamber from 1577 to 1580, and by Hunnis himself in his petition of 1583, he was never technically Master, but merely acted as deputy to Hunnis, probably even to the extent of taking all the financial risks off his

hands" (Chambers 1923: vol. 2; 36). To take over all the
risks and none of the benefits for no apparent reason,
seems inconceivable. And Chambers does not even attempt
to suggest why Hunnis would need to be thus relieved, and
why Farrant would volunteer for such a task, giving up the
group he had established and led to success; and why, in
other words, this is "pretty clear." Much more reasonable is Hillebrand's view, which accepts the evidence of
(1) the records of regular payments to Farrant as Master
of the Chapel, (2) the checque book entry of 1569 (rein-
statement), (3) Farrant's description of himself in his
will as a Gentleman of the Chapel, (4) Hunnis' chronological order of the masters (in his 1583 petition to the Queen
for raise in salary) in which he lists Farrant as succeeding
him, and (5) the Earl of Leicester's letter of recommenda-
tion, stating that Hunnis meant to rehearse the children
"in like sort as his predecessor did,"—which accepts all
this as proving that from 1569 until 1576 and later, Farrant was actually both a Gentleman of the Chapel and Master of Windsor, and that he was Master of the Chapel
while Hunnis was in temporary retirement. Hillebrand
finds that these are obvious facts, but can offer no explanation for them (Hillebrand 1926: 94-95). Harbage re-
states Chambers' suggestion more realistically, but without proof. He feels that the two companies joined forces
to combat the Paul's Boys, who were enjoying increasing
success (Harbage 1952: 37). As supporting evidence he
quotes the number of performances at Court between 1559
and 1582 as 28 for the Paul's Boys and a total of 23 for
the Windsor and Chapel groups together. There are several troubles with these figures. First, the Children of
Windsor did not exist until 1567, and consequently their
performances before that date compare rather unfavorably
with those of the extant Paul's Boys. Secondly, there is
no evidence whatsoever that there was an increase in the
number of productions of the two groups after they acquired
their theatre, especially considering that with that event
the Children of Windsor disappeared. And this is probably

149

the most important fact Harbage disregards, namely, that
after the "coalition" was born, two of the four participants,
the Children of Windsor and Hunnis, were lost from view,
and only Farrant remained with the Children of the Chapel.
I am not, of course, in a position to provide the correct
answer, but I would suggest that since Hunnis' biography
appeared just before the publication of Feuillerat 1908,
the events of his life should be examined in the light of the
new data. Similarly, a biography of Farrant should be attempted. As a result of these two studies the confusing
relationship between the two men and the two companies
might be clarified.

### Decline after Farrant

After the death of their Master, the Children of the
Chapel kept right on producing plays. Their next performance took place Shrove Tuesday (February 5), 1581,
within ten weeks of Farrant's death. The following season,
on December 31 and Shrove Tuesday (February 27), 1582,
two unnamed plays were performed under a new master,
also unknown. Only in the second season does Hunnis'
name appear, with the presentation of A Game of Cardes
on St. Stephen's day (December 26), 1582. With this
schedule in mind we cannot escape two conclusions: the
Children had to have a master and they had to have a rehearsal hall. The lack of any break in the schedule after
Farrant's death would further suggest that both the "new"
master and the working conditions (i. e. rehearsal hall)
were familiar. No new master, unfamiliar with the system of play production employed by the children's groups
could have prepared for a performance in two months.
Moreover, we have earlier, with some modification, accepted Hillebrand's suggestion that the troupe had no rehearsal hall other than the rooms at Blackfriars. That
Ann (Bower) Farrant appealed to Sir William Moore within a month of her husband's death to permit a sublease of
the premises, supports my opinion that the children were
already practicing there (Wallace 1912: 153).[12] Had this

150

not been so, she would much more likely have requested
a suspension of the lease and moved to their Greenwich house. But the theatre had probably proved too good
a business to be given up, and therefore she was willing to
legalize Hunnis' use of the premises. We must also remember that both her father and husband had been masters
of the children, and that she must have known Hunnis pretty
well too, whether or not he actually cooperated with Farrant at the Blackfriars. Therefore a transaction in which
she would have helped legally and been helped financially
would be most natural. For these reasons I assume that
it was Hunnis who took over the management of the Children and the theatre immediately upon Farrant's death, and
that he presented the three unnamed plays preceding The
Game of Cardes (Hillebrand 1926: 99). As Moore did not
answer the widow's request, she seems to have sold the
lease to Hunnis anyway, who, to make sure that he would
be able to stay at Blackfriars, asked the Earl of Leicester
to support his endeavor. The Earl did so in a letter dated
September 19, 1581 (Wallace 1912: 154). The lease was
finally settled on December 20, by which time Hunnis had
introduced one John Newman into the negotiations. Why
and whence this partner came, and what his function was
are not known. Though the Children continued to present
plays, we have several signs that doom was near. From
Moore's notes (dated 1585-1586) we know that the lease
passed from Hunnis and Newman to "Evans whoe sold his
interest to the Erle of Oxforde whoe gave his interest to
Lyllie and the title thus was posted over from one to
another from me Contrarie to the said Condicion" i. e.
that the lease was non-transferable (Wallace 1912: 176).
Therefore, Moore took the case to Court (adding the com-
plaints mentioned previously) but the proceedings were
very slow. Still, Ann Farrant and her sublessees were
all very much afraid of losing their property, and started
a legal war against each other. This is another indication
that the possession of the theatre was worth the effort.
But at the same time, toward the end of 1583, Hunnis

turned to the Queen with a petition. He cited increased trouble and "the pryces of thinges present to the tyme past", (nothing new under the sun!) as a reason for a raise (ibid. 156-157). We do not know whether this petition had the desired result, just as we do not know the final verdict in the Newman and Hunnis vs. Farrant suit (ibid. 160-168). We know, however, that Moore finally regained possession at the end of the Easter term, 1584.

The chaos became complete, it seems, just before the explosion. Corresponding to Moore's statement about the passing around of the lease, we see that the two plays which were among our first evidence for the existence of the First Blackfriars Theatre: Lyly's Campaspe and Sapho and Phao were presented at Court New Year's Day and Shrove Tuesday (March 3) 1584 respectively, by the "Earl of Oxford his seruantes," Lyly being the payee on both occasions. It should be remembered that, while giving the same dates, the title pages of these two plays name "her Maiesties Children and the Children [boys] of Pauls" as performers. Does this mean that the Children of the Chapel operated together with Paul's Boys at the Blackfriars Theatre and appeared at Court under the Earl's name, while he (or one of his friends, Evans or Lyly) held the lease of the building? Westcote, the Master of Pauls, died early in 1582, and not until 1587 did these boys, with their new Master, Thomas Gyles, appear at Court—at least not under their own name. Evans, who held the lease for a while (and who was to have a more important part in the Second Blackfriars Theatre) was called "deer friend" in Westcote's will, was a good friend of the Earl, and would have been a logical tie between the Paul's Boys and the Earl's own group (Hillebrand 1926: 135). But we do not know how Hunnis fits into this operation. Especially since between the two above-mentioned dates, the Children of the Chapel presented two plays independently, on January 6 and February 2, the second play being Peele's Arraignment of Paris, and the name of Hunnis does not appear.

It is even more puzzling that, having been evicted from the Blackfriars, Henry Evans is recorded as payee for "Children of Therle of Oxford," who presented The History of Agamemnon and Ulysses on St. John's day (December 27) 1584. Then on New Year's day 1585 the servants of the Earl presented "feates of Actiuity and vawtinge" (obviously not dramatic "Actiuity"), the payee being one Simons, who had appeared with similar "ffeates of Actiuitye and Tomblinge" as one of "Lord Straunge his servauntes" two years earlier on the same night.[13]

I believe that for the final clarification of this crucial period, a thorough investigation into the whole web of theatrical activity going on under the Earl of Oxford's name is necessary. The hypotheses advanced so far are unsatisfactory. Wallace's theory is that the Earl bought the lease of Blackfriars because he believed in Lyly's literary ability, and this theatre was to make a dramatist of him, which it did (Wallace 1912: 168-172).[14] Since the plays required a large cast, the Paul's Boys were called to help out the resident Chapel Children. The trouble is that Wallace quotes the number of actors as 28 for Campaspe and 17 for Sapho and Phao, and forgets the possibility of doubling. According to my calculation, Campaspe could have been done with 18, and Sapho and Phao with 11 or 12 actors. This means that the boys of the Chapel could have presented the latter without outside help. Wallace, however, goes on to declare it "patent" that the Paul's boys came into the affair because while Gyles did not attempt dramatic performances, he was paid for his services by the Blackfriars managers. Of course, there is no record of this. Wallace also takes it for granted that the plays presented by the Chapel alone, between the performances of the combined company, were under Hunnis' direction—for which we also lack any proof whatever. That Hunnis could and would have gone on with his original group of children after having sold the lease and handed over the management of the combined company to Lyly, who had never before had anything to do with theatre—is rather

hard to believe. To train the same group of children
simultaneously under two masters in two different repertoires would have been a practical impossibility. And what
satisfactory arrangement, financial or otherwise, could
have been made about performances at the Blackfriars?
Lyly presenting the combined company one night and Hunnis leading the Children of the Chapel contingent the next,
with the lease in the hands of Evans—this certainly seems
absurd.

Again, Hillebrand offers a more logical arrangement
(Hillebrand 1926: 133-136). He emphasizes the apparent
understanding between Evans, Lyly and Oxford, and believes that Hunnis' letter to the Queen is indicative of his
having been dropped from the enterprise. Pointing to
Evans' connection with Westcote, Hillebrand suggests that
Evans secured the lease in order to take over the enterprise following his friend's death, since Gyles did not appear to want to. The Paul's Boys, then, would have been
called by the name of Oxford because of the Earl's patronage over them, as well as over Lyly, whose plays (possibly
more than the two we know of, at these premises so ardently
fought-for) they presented. On the occasions when the
cast was too large (the Paul's company numbering only
ten) the Chapel was called in to assist. It is true that, as
Hillebrand says, this scheme explains Evans' becoming
involved in the enterprise, the cooperation of the two
groups, the independent ventures of the Chapel at Court,
and Gabriel Harvey's "ironical dig" at Lyly, calling him
"Vicemaster at Poules;" though particulary on the third
count I would not call the solution a happy one (Hillebrand
1926: 136). For where did the independent Chapel operate?
It should be remembered that Hillebrand's position concerning the Children of the Chapel's having lost their
previous rehearsal-hall is more forbidding than my modi-
fied suggestion.

But there are other questions that remain unanswered
by Hillebrand's theory. Why, if Evans had dramatic aspirations of his own, did he not take over the direction at

Paul's, and produce his own plays as all masters did?
Why did he leave all the creative work to Lyly? Then, if
Paul's Company became that of Oxford, why did it shortly
cease? Surely the Earl of Oxford could have made arrangements with Moore if he was bent on making the road free
for Lyly to become a major playwright. It is also surprising to find the Earl, himself a playwright, supporting
Lyly's aspirations rather than having his own plays
performed.[15]

All this puzzling activity came to an abrupt end with
the final verdict of the Court, which gave Sir William
Moore possession of the rooms that had housed the First
Blackfriars Theatre for a period of more than seven years.


## II. ASPECTS OF THE OPERATION
## OF THE FIRST BLACKFRIARS THEATRE

Having followed the history of the First Blackfriars
Theatre from its beginnings through its decline, I will now
give a picture of its operation. The problems to be considered are those relating to the theatre's plant, audience
accommodation, music and acting, repertoire and staging.

### Plant

The rooms in which Farrant established his theatre
were located in two adjoining buildings in the Blackfriars
precinct. These buildings originally housed the kitchen
and the dining halls of the old priory. After the dissolu-
tion of the monastery they were used for meetings of
Parliament, various functions of the Revels Office, and
for private residences. All our evidence concerning the
physical conditions of the theatre is contained in leases
and other legal documents held by the Moore family and
printed by Feuillerat and by Wallace (Feuillerat 1913:
19-34; Wallace 1912: 131-177).

From the lease it is clear that Farrant rented six
rooms on the upper floor of which two were in the northern

building and together measured 46 1/2' x 25'. The northern
building abutted on the southern one, which contained Farrant's other four rooms, together measuring 110' x 22'.
These are all the facts we know. As can be expected conjectural diagrams based on such scanty evidence differ
considerably. Adams lines up the six rooms on a common
wall, and he indicates no staircase between the southern
and northern rooms (Adams 1917-a: 82). Chambers on the
other hand presents the rooms as not having a common
wall, although on the same level, and he indicates a descending flight of stairs at the juncture of the two buildings,
separating the two northern rooms from the four southern
ones (Chambers 1923: vol. 2; 504-505). It is to be re-
gretted that Sir Edmund does not comment on Adams' diagram. The separating stairs are mentioned in the lease
and must have rendered the combined use of the six rooms
as a playhouse impossible, even if they had a common
wall for which the documents do not present evidence.
Feuillerat probably did not realize this and suggested that
the northern two rooms had fine dimensions for a conveniently spacious stage, to which the actors had easy access
by a flight of stairs descending into a room also rented by
Farrant (Feuillerat 1912: 84-85). This suggestion implies that the four other rooms were used as the auditorium
and could accommodate a large audience. Adams is opposed to Feuillerat's suggestion because he finds 110' x
22' to be absurd dimensions for an auditorium. He does
not point out, however, that the staircase separated the
two sections of the theatre supposed by Feuillerat. According to Adams both stage and auditorium were contained in the two northern rooms (Adams 1917-a: 101).
This would imply that only the partition between these
two rooms was torn down. We remember, however, that
Moore complained that Farrant tore down several partitions and that it was Adams who called attention to the
probable reason why Moore complained: his lodging adjoined the theatre (see above, p.145 & n7). Thus it is
surprising to find Adams implying that only the one

156

partition was pulled down. The fact that Lawrence esti-
mates the number of seats to have been 240 indicates his
agreement with Adams (Lawrence 1912: 233). In order to
seat an audience of 240 (a minimum of 3 1/2 sq. ft. has to
be counted per person) and to allow for at least one narrow
aisle the length of the auditorium, about 900 sq. ft. are
needed—i. e. , and area of 36' x 25'. That leaves us with a
stage area of 10' x 25' which must be narrowed, by the
establishment of a tiring house on either or both sides, to
about 10' x 15'. These measurements, as we will see,
would not have allowed the action and the stage machinery
indicated by the surviving plays and other evidence. We
should not forget that the custom of sitting on the stage
would have further restricted any acting area. While a
smaller stage (7' 10 1/2"x 15') was probably used between
1557 and 1568, as Charles T. Prouty's discoveries about
Trinity Hall (the only known indoor playhouse prior to the
First Blackfriars Theatre) indicate, it was small only because of the limited space available for the whole playhouse (Prouty 1953). It would seem quite foolish of Farrant to have sufficient room at hand and not make use of
it. For this reason Harbage's conception of the stage
being set up in the end of the four narrow rooms seems
much more realistic. This way he gets an auditorium of
22' x 75' and a maximum seating capacity of 400, while
the remaining 35' x 22' provide the actors with a convenient stage and tiring room (Harbage 1952: 43).

Both Adams and Lawrence seem to be justified in re-
jecting Feuillerat's theory that galleries were built all a-
round the Blackfriars auditorium as they were when royal
or private halls were temporarily converted into playhouses (Feuillerat 1912: 84). Such construction would
undoubtedly have caused Moore to protest further viola-
tion of the lease. Moreover, it is not probable that Farrant had the means for such an investment.

Lawrence was the only writer on the subject who
thought about the use of the rooms supposedly not converted into the theatre. He thought that Farrant had to

live on the premises to qualify his playhouse as private. [16] Occupation would be necessary, according to Lawrence, because the "Act of Common Council" of December 6, 1575, regulated all acting within the city except "anie playes ... or shewes to be plaied or shewed in the pryvate hous" on occasion of "anie marriage, assembly of frrendes, or otherlyke cawse" (Lawrence 1912: 231). But as we have seen, there was no need for such precaution since the Blackfriars precinct was outside the jurisdiction of the city. The term "private" as associated with playhouses, may safely be taken to mean "intimate, " as distinguished from "common" or "public" (Adams 1917a: 94). Physically the distinction between the public and private theatre lay respectively in the difference between a roofed, rectangular auditorium with its seated pit, and an unroofed circular pit for standees. The private theatre had to be artificially lighted and heated (since it performed throughout the winter season), and catered to an audience select in respect to quality as well as quantity.

## Audience Accommodation

It has been pointed out (above, p. 146) how the prospective audience and the location of the theatre determined each other. That is, by settling in the most fashionable district of London, Farrant created a theatre of the courtier class. His intention was a consequence of his belonging to the Royal Household and having in view the presentation of the Children at Court before Elizabeth. Had the purpose of the new enterprise been purely out-of-Court performances, and not the improvement of the troupe and the greater favour of the Queen, the group still could not have switched easily to a different audience with a different taste. With a select audience of about 400, the First Blackfriars Theatre was what we would today call a "chamber–theatre." This means, it provided an atmosphere of intimacy, built upon the foundation of established tradition, took the road of experimentation, introduced a series of innovations and cleared the way for further developments.

A very important practice initiated at Farrant's theatre — one that is still with us — was to seat the whole audience. Among conditions most likely to have led to the establishment of the seated pit were the following: (1) no galleries could be built in the Blackfriars rooms (see above, p. 157); (2) due to the low ceiling a stage six feet high was out of the question, and a much lower one would have prevented the rear portion of a standing audience from seeing much of the stage; (3) the audience was composed of courtiers used to being seated at court performances as well as at public theatres; (4) admission rates above those at the public theatres were necessary to keep the playhouse going, and for higher prices the spectators would justly expect better accommodation. It is possible that Farrant also had in mind what became the most important result of total seating: the improvement of the general atmosphere. The seated pit put an end to the constant commotion customary at the public theatres, reduced the capacity of the house, and provided the audience with greater comfort. Thus it helped the theatre achieve a formal, dignified and sophisticated atmosphere. A more comfortable and less distracting arrangement might have induced the audience to make an increased mental effort, challenging both author and performer in the use of more subtle techniques. Such commonly disregarded conveniences may seem trivial; yet we cannot dismiss them if we are to understand the emergence of artificial comedy. Terms used to describe the seated pit, such as "seat of judgement," or "glorious tribunal," have meaning only when we take into consideration the changed mental attitude of a seated audience (Lawrence 1921).[17]
Another innovation in the accommodation of the audience is the custom of sitting on the stage. It has received somewhat more scholarly attention than the seated pit. The influence of this custom on Elizabethan staging was more direct and more specific than that of the seated pit, yet its beginnings have so far not been successfully dated or accounted for. Before the story of the First Blackfriars

Theatre became known, Wallace compiled over half a dozen references from between the years 1598 and 1604, to people being seated on the stage (Wallace 1908: 130-134).[18] He was attempting to prove that the custom originated with and was an exclusive feature of Burbage's Blackfriars Theatre. Pointing out the rashness of Wallace's assumption, Professor Baskerville calls our attention to the fact that Davies' Epigrams (see footnote #18) containing such reference are certainly two and possibly four years earlier than Wallace suggests; that Burbage's Blackfriars was not then in operation; that not all references specify Blackfriars as the home of the custom and, indeed, that one mentions Paul's specifically; and that these references therefore "only lead us to infer that the custom prevailed there /Blackfriars/ before 1603-4" and do not prove that it originated there (Baskerville 1911: 586). With the help of contemporary reports of Court and school performances, T. S. Graves tried to find the origin of the practice of sitting on the stage in earlier times. But the passage that to him "perhaps implies" that Henry VIII sat on the stage in 1527 states only that "all actors, one after the other, presented themselves to the King," upon the conclusion of the play—a circumstance suggesting an early precursor of the modern curtain call rather than Henry's sitting on the stage (Graves 1914: 106 &n.). Reference to prologues and epilogues of Lyly's plays as well as to the ending of Peele's Arraignment of Paris (where the Queen was handed the golden ball) can readily be dismissed, for they indicate only the proximity of the Queen to the stage or that the actors approached her.

In this respect, however, the performances at Cambridge and Oxford in the years 1564 and 1566 respectively are of greater importance. In an English description (see Appendix) of the Cambridge performance it seems that the word "stage" was used alternately to mean the acting platform and a platform for spectators. Therefore, when we read that "From the quire door unto the large stage was made as 'twere a bridge rayled no [sic] both sides;

for the Queen's Grace to go to the stage: which was
straightly kept," we cannot be sure that it was the acting
platform she ascended.  In a Latin report on the Oxford
performance of 1566, John Bereblock is at once more
clear and more ambiguous.  He also describes a bridge,
supported by props, through which "the Queen might hasten
by an easy ascent to the play (spectacula) when it was ready"
(Durand 1905: 505).  The use of the Latin word spectacula
does not seem to leave any doubt as to where the Queen
was hastening.  In a passage immediately following, however, we have an example of the confused usage of termini
technici both in Elizabethan Latin and in modern English.

> In the upper part of the hall, where it looks to
> the west, a stage is built, large and lofty, and
> many steps high... (theatrum excitatur magnum
> et erectum, gradibusque multis excelsum)
>
> On each side of the stage magnificent palaces
> and well equipped houses are built up for the
> actors in the comedies and for the masked
> persons... (Ex utroque scenae latera comoe-
> dis ac personatis magnificia palatia aedesque
> apparatissime extruuntur) (ibid: 505. Nichols
> 1788: vol. 1. Oxford 1566; 41. Italics mine).

The two words, both translated "stage," do not necessarily have the same meaning.  While scena unmistakably refers to the platform on which scenery was constructed
and the actors performed, theatrum is more a term con-
noting audience, one of its meanings being an assemblage
of spectators.  Besides, the use of the word gradibusque
is suspicious for two reasons:  1) it is not probable that
the side of the stage towards the audience was accessible
by a flight of stairs; 2) in Italian theatres of the Renaissance the step-by-step rising seats of the audience were
termed gradi.  Though not conclusively proving that
theatrum actually referred to the auditorium, this reasoning at least calls attention to the ambiguity of the Latin

terms and to the puzzlement of a modern scholar in his attempt to translate them correctly.

Though the above paragraphs reduce the proofs of Graves to theories, one still could assume that in a theatre as strongly court-oriented as Farrant's the example for sitting on the stage was set by court practice. Had the Queen sat on the stage, it is likely that in her absence the most distinguished visitors of the courtier-theatre would have been flattered with a similar privilege and would have willingly paid a high price for it. Had sitting on the stage not been established at court performances, we may still argue from analogy that Elizabeth sat on her dais in the middle of the hall, where everyone could see her and where she had the best "sightlines." Thus a desire for social distinction and Elizabethan vanity rather than overcrowded conditions must have been the primary cause of this custom (Graves 1914: 109; Lawrence 1912: 234-5; Harbage 1952: 45-7).[19] Doubtless, the shape of the auditorium would make both being seen and seeing difficult. Hence the position of those sitting on the stage was enviable from every point of view: they were seen and they could most closely observe the actors who now acted primarily to them and whose performance they could appraise most intimately. Thereby they entitled themselves to authoritative comment both during and after the presentation of the play.

Sitting on the stage was beneficial because it effected a further refinement of taste. At the same time we have to realize that spectators seated on what was in any case a small stage must have obstructed the actors considerably and have made scene changes extremely difficult.[20] That the custom was tolerated in spite of interference, was due to the additional price of these "twelvepenny stools" (Harbage 1952: 45).

## Music and Acting

We should now turn our attention to an innovation that transformed play and performance alike: the use of music

as an integrated production element. The addition of music
was not unrelated to the changes just discussed; rather they
prepared the atmosphere necessary for its employment.
Nor was music alien to the origin of the private theatre.
Court entertainment was fundamentally of musical character: that is why the choirboys became part of it. When,
under the direction of their masters, who were singers,
musicians, composers themselves, the Children entered
into a theatrical enterprise, their musical background can
be expected to have determined the nature of their performance. A look into the surviving plays performed by
them will show the use of music and song to be indicated
by numerous lines and stage directions, many of which
are followed by the lyrics themselves. Other songs, once
separated from their plays, have been found and placed in
the structure of their plays on grounds of internal evidence.
That plays were preceded by an hour long concert and that
they utilized both instrumental and vocal music between
acts, in addition to songs and mood music built into the
play, justify the assertion that the private playhouse was
"almost as much concert hall as theatre" (Harbage 1952:
45; Lawrence 1930: 424).

The music for the overtures and interludes has not
survived, but from the few extant songs we can see that
they were intended to support the poignancy of tragic and
pathetic situations by means of a solo contralto voice accompanied by strings. The lyrics employ a number of
mechanical devices to achieve dramatic effect; i.e., re-
petitions of names, words or phrases such as "Now I die,"
"I sigh and sob," or exclamations like "ah, ah, alas."
The pathos which the author was unable to convey through
the lyrics had to be supplemented by the composer (Arkwright 1913-4: 135). This is why the First Blackfriars
Theatre is the first one we know of to produce plays in
which songs, dances and musical interludes were not only
customary but essential. There, far from being incidental, the music became the unifying, integrating element and
the key to further developments both in acting and in
playwrighting.

It is important to note that this use of music emerged together with the acting style we find linked with it. The pathos of these plays might easily have become ridiculous for a sophisticated audience had music not accompanied certain lines. The introduction of music helped avoid monotonous declamation by the Children and gave them opportunity to take advantage of their superior musical ability and training. That pathos became acceptable in the musical vein does not mean that the presentation became less theatrical; it merely acquired a different, a more pleasing artificiality. Music also served to produce gentleness, lightness, subtlety, charm; qualities that were also brought into the performance by the age of the actors. Melody, rhythm and grace came to dominate scripts and performances alike. The discrepancy of the husky, bellowing hero confronted with a little lad-lady has disappeared: both hero and heroine are in their early teens. The little actors were supplied with a number of crutches; gorgeous costumes, elaborate scenery, fancy hand-properties became as essential in creating an atmosphere on stage as songs, choruses and dances. With this overall change of style, the boy actors proved to be superb vehicles for increasingly witty, satiric and topical lines. Every reference to friendship, intrigue and particularly to sex could be loaded with double and triple meanings.

### Repertoire

The most obvious difference between the repertoires of the public (adult) and the private (children) companies is a topical one. While the plays of the public companies were drawing on the romance tradition and on English history, the titles of the Children's plays indicate a classical interest with a moralistic-didactic orientation. When we add this topical difference to the numerous innovations discussed above – i. e., the seated pit, sitting on the stage, music as an integrated production element, and the acting style – it is not hard to see how artificiality, stylization and subtlety culminate in the plays of John Lyly

under the Earl of Oxford's patronage of the Blackfriars
Theatre.

Not much can be said about the repertoire of the First
Blackfriars Theatre. None of the plays we know Richard
Farrant produced (Ajax and Ulysses, Quintus Fabius,
Xerxes, Mutius Scaevola, The historie of Loyaltie and
beautie, The historie of Alucius) have survived.21 Lyly's
Alexander and Campaspe, and Sapho and Phao, and Peele's
Arraignment of Paris are well enough known to make a
discussion of their literary qualities unnecessary in this
context.

There is, however, another play of interest: The
Wars of Cyrus. Though it was probably never performed
at Court (since we have no records of its being paid for,
and since its title page does not boast of an appearance
before the Queen) the play is pertinent to our discussion
of Blackfriars because it is supposed to have been written
by Richard Farrant. It was printed in 1594 and the title
page claimed it to have been performed by the Children
of the Chapel. This claim dates the play before 1584, in
which year the Children ceased, for a sixteen year period,
to produce plays. However, the play's first editor in our
time, Dr. Keller, considered it an imitation of Tamburlaine
and thus dated it after 1587 (Brawner 1942: 10). The first
to attribute The Wars of Cyrus to Farrant was W. J. Lawrence. His attribution was prompted by a discovery of
several worldly songs of Farrant. Among them was one
beginning "Alas, ye salt sea gods" which Arkwright had
previously assumed to belong to a lost play called presumably Panthea and Abradatas. Lawrence connected
the song with The Wars of Cyrus not only because its
heroine is named Panthea and because the song fits into
the play at a point where she mourns her dead husband,
Abradatas; but also because he thought that "anyone of
judgement who compares 'Alas ye salt sea gods' with
The Warres of Cyrus will have little difficulty in deter-
mining that both were emanations from the one mind"
(Lawrence 1921). 22

Besides this song –play relationship and the 1584 ter-
minal year just mentioned, further evidence for Farrant's
authorship is the fact that the play is not an imitation of
Marlowe. As Brawner points out, the play is not a con-
queror play at all, because not Cyrus but Panthea is its
central character. Furthermore, the prologue designates
the play as "tragicke" (ll. 11&16) and only with Panthea
as the central figure can it be tragic. In addition the
theme of the faithful captive woman seems to be a recur-
ring one at the Blackfriars Theatre, The Wars of Cyrus
being followed by the Historie of Alucius and finally by
Lyly's Campaspe. Finally, the play must antedate Lyly's
period at Blackfriars, because the prologue appeals to
"gentle gentlemen" who are "worthie to iudge;" and the
author could not have expected his courtly audience to
approve of the play – one lacking grace, charm, subtlety
and elegance – unless he preceded Lyly. Grouping all the
above facts together, Brawner concludes The Wars of
Cyrus was definitely Farrant's play and in all likelihood
the premier performance of the First Blackfriars Theatre (Brawner 1942: 11-19).

Looking at the play, then, as one of 1576/7 we must
grant that it is rather a good one in comparison with
others of its time. Its blank verse rolls much more
smoothly and has much more finish and variety than the
verse of either Gorboduc or Iocasta.[23] The subplot, the
story of the inconstant Gobryas, is very skillfully fitted
into the main structure of the play (see especially ll. 368-
373 and 580-583). The disguise device, later to be exploited by Shakespeare, gets a good start in English
theatre; succinct dialogue techniques appear (see e.g.
ll. 97-99); and the character of Panthea is made distinctly
engaging. Songs and music (later deleted from the printed
play) find their way into the script to round out the pathetic atmosphere. All in all, it is a play interesting to read
even four centuries later and must have fascinated its
original audience when presented with all the resources
of the Blackfriars Theatre. Why it did not attain a Court

performance, we do not know; but Farrant must have been
rather bent on presenting the general theme of The Wars
of Cyrus before the Queen, for one of the later plays given
by the Children of the Chapel, Alucius, also revolved a-
round the sufferings of a faithful captive woman (Brawner
1942: 55-56).

Staging
The notion of a bare stage in the Elizabethan theatre
is now defunct. A glance into the Revels Accounts shows
that even as early as the period of the First Blackfriars
Theatre a lavish supply of scenery units, costumes and
stage properties was used to realize on stage the poets'
dramatic visions.[24]
Most of the Revels information, although not specifically connected with the Blackfriars Theatre clearly indicates that original stage directions and allusions in the
text of plays to Sybilla's cave, Apelles' studio, the Poplar
tree, the Euphrates' "sedgie bank" do not refer to imaginary scenery. In respect to general stage form, although
the tradition of medieval staging was very much in evidence,
suggestions pointing to exclusive use of the polyscenic stage
of juxtaposition are probably exaggerated. We know that
Italian influence, exerted through both English and Italian
travelers, was particularly strong in this period and extended to every field of knowledge. Therefore, it is not
surprising that Rothwell finds ample evidence for methods resembling those of Serlio both in scenery construction and in perspective painting (Rothwell 1953: 101-9).
It has been argued that Serlio's influence could not have
been felt, since the English translation of his Treatise
appeared only in 1611. But a reference to "Old Vitruvius
(Leo Baptista) and Serlo [sic]" in Harrison's Description
of Britain and England (1577) proves that either the original
edition (1545) of Serlio or its immediately prepared French
translation must have been known in England (Rothwell
1953: 109). Rothwell follows up this reasoning with the
perfectly justified question: "And if Harrison knew of

Serlio and Vitruvius, then why not the Revels Office, whose business it was to be au courant on such matters?" (ibid: 110).

It is safe, then, to assume that both a living medieval tradition and a significant renaissance influence were manifest in the staging methods at the Blackfriars Theatre. Examination of the four plays that have come down to us from the theatre's repertoire will support this assumption, because their staging requirements show strong evidence of both influences.

Medieval methods seem particularly fit for the production of the earliest Blackfriars play, The Wars of Cyrus. The majority of the scenes take place in the Persian camp, represented by at least two practical tents: one, in which Panthea and Nicosia are discovered at the beginning of the play and in which Panthea is later found asleep (III, 2), and another one in which Araspas is lying in bed (II, 2). The second locale, the Assyrian Court, is definitely used three times; and we may suppose that another scene, mentioning Gobryas' castle in Assyria but otherwise unlocalized (II, 4), is acted pretty close to the Assyrian Court. There remain two scenes on the "bankes of Euphrates," in one of which the proximity of Assyria is suggested by the entrance of Antiochus, king of Assyria. We can picture without difficulty Cyrus' camp set up on one side of the stage, Antiochus' Court on the other, and the river into which the distressed Panthea leaps represented by a trap opening, when needed, centerstage. There is indicated also a poplar tree on the banks of the Euphrates, in the shade of which Libanio dies (III, 3).

The next play chronologically, The Arraignment of Paris, seems to require quite different staging. The action takes place in a rather unified setting, in which minor changes occur during the course of the play. Flora's description of ".... these fieldes, and groves and sweetest bowres/ Bestrewed and deckt with partie collored flowers ... " (ll. 90-106), reminds us of Serlio's satyric scene, though it does not prove the author's familiarity with that design. If we trust an allusion to the "entrauce of the bowre" (l. 144), Pallas' suggestion to the gods, "Retire we to Dianes bowre" (l. 390), and a stage direction about a company of at least nine gods "being set in Dianaes bower" (i. 915), there was a practical bower on stage. Of the trees, at least the poplar under which Paris and Oenone sit together (l. 271), must also have been practical. Neither the greenery nor the properties referred to in the lines and stage directions require facilities beyond those of the Revels Office.

In respect to hand properties, Iuno has "her crounet and her mace" (l. 116), Pallas "her helme, her launce, her Gorgons head" (l. 122), Venus "Her dayntie fan and twentie other thinges" (1.131), Mercury had to have a pair of "winges" so he could "dare wage" them (l. 659). And there was, of course, the golden apple or ball, around which the whole plot revolves, and which is finally delivered "to the Queenes owne hands" (l. 1344). We even know a little of the costumes: Iuno wore yellow (l. 118), Pallas red (l. 121), Venus blue (l. 129), and Paris green (l. 711). The wonders of machinery included a "storme being past of thunder and lightning" (l. 382), "a Tree of gold laden with Diadems and Crownes of golde" that rose from the stage floor and sunk back (l. 488, 495), and "Pluto [who] ascēdeth from below in his chaire" (l. 902).

For a performance of Alexander and Campaspe, a medieval type polyscenic stage is most feasible, even on the small stage of the Blackfriars Theatre. Most of the action takes place on the market place, but the interior as well as the exterior of Apelles' studio is just as important. The very first scene of the play has the suburbs as its locale, and one or two scenes may take place in or around Alexander's palace. What is needed, then, is one practical mansion or pavilion in dominant position, with curtains to close it off when necessary.[25] This is Apelles' studio, the interior of which figures prominently in III, 3 and is used at least two other times. Several scenes are placed right in front of the studio, into which exits are made.

Two flats on either side of the stage suffice to depict a
city gate (for the suburb scene) and a palace, respectively.
Diogenes' tub can be located rather close to the city gate,
thereby establishing its distance from Alexander's palace.
The market scenes utilize the general acting area, either
one or the other side of it (sometimes starting at one side
and continuing to the other), depending on whether or not
the presence of Diogenes is required.

Our fourth play, upon first glance, also suggests the
use of medieval mansions. On second thought, however,
the impossibility of such a solution will be revealed. In
the lines of Sapho and Phao three distinct, practical locales are alluded to. Therefore, the representation of
Sybilla's cave, Sapho's bedchamber, and Vulcan's forge
is indispensible. The use of the last can be proved with
certainty only in IV, 4, where "The Song in making the
Arrowes" (1.33), and Vulcan's "Heere Venus, I have
finished these arrowes by arte" (1.49) indicate the actual
manufacturing was acted out on stage. Venus' decision
in V, 1 to "tarye for Cupid at the forge" (1.51), is no proof
that she is already there.

Sybilla's cave is doubtlessly used in II, 1, where Phao
says: "And loe! behold Sybilla in the mouth of her caue"
(1.12-13). The next scene must be the same, for Phao
does not exit until the end of II.2, when everyone leaves
the stage. Because of the group exit, II.3 should be located elsewhere. II.4 seems to combine the use of both
the exterior and the interior of the cave, for upon Sybilla's
"Come in" (1.42) Phao continues to converse with her
without change of locale. The cave is not then used until
the last scene of the play, when Sybilla again "sitteth in
her caue" (1.2).

Though Acts III and IV center around Sapho's bedchamber, III, 1 must be at some distance from Sapho to
justify Eugenia's coming to fetch Mileta. The transfer
to the chamber occurs only in III.3. The use of this chamber causes some confusion. Curtains are drawn and with-
drawn to cover or to reveal Sapho. Rothwell takes Sapho's

exclamation "you keepe the chamber too hotte!" (l. 80) to indicate "definitely that the chamber, and not the bed alone, is curtained" (Rothwell 1953: 140). This conclusion, however, contradicts an earlier sequence, where Mileta's question, "Shall we draw the curtaines, whilest you gyue your selfe to slumber?" (l. 29) draws the answer from Sapho, "Doe, but departe not" (l. 31). After "Shee falleth asleepe, The Curtaines drawne, " (l. 36) the two ladies stay right there in pleasant conversation while Sapho sleeps and after she awakes. They must, then, definitely be in the room. Further complications arise in the next series of scenes. Phao, after being bidden "Farewell for this time" by Sapho (III, 4, l. 85), does not exit but has a short dialogue with Venus, who, after also bidding him farewell, pays a visit to Sapho (in the next scene, IV. 1) without first exiting. At the end of this scene the stage direction says, "Exit Sapho." However, we know her to be in bed; and after a scene between Venus and Cupid (IV. 2) Sapho is still in bed ("Draw the curtain" IV. 3, l. 95).

However indispensible the three locales just discussed are, only half of the scenes of the play can be connected with them. The rest of the action is unlocalized; a street in Syracuse would fit them all, with the exception of the very first scene of the play. This is the so called ferry scene. Though judged by Bond and Rothwell to take place in Syracuse, Venus' line "we will to Syracusa" (l. 31) and the description of the ferry as one "that bendeth to Syracusa" (l. 50-52) indicate a considerable distance from the place of destination.

It would be more than difficult to use medieval staging for this play, for it would mean placing three sizable mansions, one of which is only used once, on a small stage; moreover, most of the action disregards all three.

With these staging problems still in mind, let us now consider the following. William E. Miller called attention to a note appended by Abraham Fleming to his translation of Vergil's Eclogues and Georgics (1589) in which Fleming seems to indicate the existence of periaktoi at the First

171

Blackfriars (Miller 1959). The note is attached to the word "curtens" in the English rendering of Georgics, III. v. 22-25, and reads as follows:

> or hangings: this seemeth to be ment of that
> kind of pagent, called versilis, siue versatilis,
> and not of the other named ductilis, which was
> drawne, read of their seuerall sorts in Servi.
> & Vitruvius lib. 5. this deuise was not unlike
> the motion of late years to be seen in the blacke
> friers.

The gloss of Servius Grammaticus to the same lines in Vergil includes this definition of the device:

> versilis tunc erat, cum subito tota machinis
> quibusdam convertebatur et aliam picturae
> faciem ostendebat.

It is the same as the periactus of Vitruvius, consisting of three-sided prisms with a locale painted on each side. The change of locale is effected by turning all prisms of a set (from two to five) at the same time.

From the reference it is clear that Fleming must have seen periaktoi at the Blackfriars. Because Fleming was a Puritan, Miller suggests that he either attended a play for non-dramatic (political) reasons or that he saw the device in the empty theatre after 1584.

The problem of how many periaktoi were used is a minor one: there could have been from two to five, but the financial status of the theatre as well as the size of the stage would suggest the former. More important, why, if periaktoi were used at the Blackfriars before 1584, is there no mention of any similar apparatus until Inigo Jones' use of them in 1605? For if periaktoi were known at Blackfriars, they must have been standard pieces of equipment at Court, and devices known to other theatres. Any answer would have to accord with concepts already expressed. If the Blackfriars was a theatre with a select audience, and if it was an experimental enterprise, the

use of periaktoi might have formed another experiment
suggested by a noble patron who saw them in Italy—but
not successful enough to be used at Court until much later.
The idea of periaktoi had ample chance to reach the
Blackfriars. A diagram in Vignola's Le due regoli di
prospettiva pratica edited by Danti and published in Rome,
1583 (just before the climax and decline of the Blackfriars
Theatre) shows a set of five periaktoi, a combination similar to that which was operated by Baldassare Lanci da
Urbino in 1569 at the Medici Court, Florence (Nagler 1960:
165). The earliest stage which changed its scenery in
this way was seen in June 1543 at Castro, Italy, and was
built by Aristotile (Bastiano) da San Gallo (1481-1551)
(Rapp 1944: 60, n).

Though Fleming's reference does not prove the use
of periaktoi at the Blackfriars conclusively, it does fit
into our picture of an experimental theatre. In addition,
it may even help resolve the confusion encountered earlier.
If we recollect the staging of the plays discussed, we see
that the use of periaktoi would not improve the staging of
The Wars of Cyrus and The Arraignment of Paris. It
could, however, heighten the effect in Alexander and
Campaspe if used on the sides of the dominant mansion or
pavilion, its three sides depicting the interior of Apelles'
studio, the market place, and the interior of Alexander's
palace, respectively. Turning finally to Sapho and Phao,
the use of periaktoi would clear up the confusion discussed
earlier. Using one sizable mansion (pavilion) that can be
closed by curtains and placing on either side of it periaktoi,
on the sides of which would be painted indications of a
street, a forest and of Sapho's bedchamber, the following
combinations would be possible: 1) periaktoi show forest
scene, open mansion has Sybilla sitting in it; 2) same sides
of periaktoi, in the open mansion Vulcan with anvil and
bellows; 3) periaktoi present street-scene, further depicted on the closed curtains of the mansion; 4) Sapho's
bedchamber on the periaktoi, mansion open containing
Sapho in bed. Whether the bed has another set of curtains,

or the curtains of the mansion are drawn while the periaktoi
still show the chamber, is immaterial.

Thus Miller's discovery concerning periaktoi can be
supported on theatrical grounds. Moreover, this addition
to our knowledge of the First Blackfriars Theatre fits in
with the basic conclusion suggested by the whole study of
its operation, namely that it was an experimental theatre,
a pioneering, pathfinding effort in all aspects of theatrical
activity—playhouse policy making, playwrighting, audience
accommodation, application of music, acting style and
production techniques.

This study, though it attempts to summarize and re-
valuate all available knowledge within its scope, can by no
means be definitive. Such an essay can only follow upon
a final clarification of mysteries in the lives of Farrant,
Hunnis, Evans, Lyly, in operations of companies such as
the Paul's Boys and the different groups under the Earl
of Oxford's patronage, and after a further examination
of the topographical, financial and legal documents relative to the First Blackfriars Theatre.

## NOTES

1. The Loseley MSS are now in the Folger Shakespeare
Library. The priority of their discovery has been argued
in the drama section of Athenaeum, 1912 (Nov. 2, 9, 23, 30)
and 1913 (Jan. 4, 11, 18).

2. See also Daily Chronicle, Dec. 22, 1911.

3. Brawner suggests (Brawner 1942: 48) that Farrant
actually served as assistant to both his father-in-law and
Richard Edwards, but there is no supporting evidence
for this.

4. All dates of performances are given according to the
Court calender in Chambers (Chambers 1923: vol. 4; 75-
101). We do not know the titles of the plays performed at

Shrovetide (February 29 –March 2) 1568, on Shrove Tuesday (February 22) 1569, on St. John's Day (December 27) 1569, and on Shrove Monday (February 26) 1571.

5.   The title "Xerxes" is not given.   The assumption is made on a notation in the Revels Accounts:   "perwigg of Heare for King xerxces syster in ffarantes playe" (Documents 1908:  244).

6.   Both letters and the lease are printed in Wallace 1912:  131 n1, n2; 132 n3.

7.   Moore's complaint is printed in Wallace 1912:  174 n2; 175-176.  As J.Q. Adams points out (Adams 1917-a: 103), Moore had cause to complain.  His home adjoined the rooms rented by Farrant.

8.   "ffrom the ffeste of Saynt Michael Tharchangell last past before the date hereof ..." reads the lease (Wallace 1912:  134).

9.   But we have record of an earlier performance: December 27, 1577.

10.  His will (in Wallace 1912:  152) was signed November 30, 1580 and probated the following March.  "a poore and sorrowfull widdowe An ffarant" signed a letter to Moore on December 25 of the same year.  DNB, however, says the entry of Farrant's death in the Cheque Book appears in both 1580 and 1581 on the same date, and quotes Hawkins' History (1833:  465) that Farrant retired to Windsor and died there in 1585.

11.  Feuillerat's description of the matter gives only half the truth:  "que faire d'une salle de spectacle sans acteurs? Fort heureusment William Hunnis intervint.  Il proposa à la veuve de prendre la location à sa charge pour continue l'oeuvre de Farrant." (Feuillerat 1910-a:  272) For one thing, the actors were there:  the Children of the Chapel. And for another, if Hunnis took over the Children, the taking over of the theatre was no charity, but business: a sine qua non of the Children as an acting group, and it

meant at least as much money for Hunnis as for the widow.

12. The various documents referred to here and below, are reprinted in Wallace 1912, in the places cited in the text.

13. No question about this part of the confusion concerning the Earl's acting troupes has been raised by any writer in connection with the First Blackfriars Theatre.

14. Here, as with Cornish, Wallace gives way to superlatives. A more restrained evaluation is put forth by Lawrence.

15. George Puttenham (Puttenham 1589: 77), after listing those who "for Tragedie ... do deserue the hyest price," goes on to note "th'Erle of Oxford and Maister Edwardes of her Maiesties Chappell for Comedy and Enterlude."

16. It must be remembered that Farrant had ten children. He had also, as his will shows, a house in Greenwich. The Master's contract, moreover, provided him with lodgings within the Royal Household. This provision was probably made so that the Master would live with his choirboys. —That the 12 Children of the Chapel (together with the 10 Farrant children) were all put up at the Blackfriars is most unlikely.

17. I have not found anyone who elaborates on the significance of this change.

18. Wallace quotes the relevant passages from Marston's What You Will and Malcontent, Middleton's A Mad World My Masters, Percy's The Faery Pastorall, Ben Jonson's Everyman Out of His Humour and Cynthia's Revels, Chapman's All Fools; and Epigram 3 of Sir John Davies, which he dates 1598.

19. Overcrowded conditions were suggested by Lawrence, but Harbage has argued effectively for slim attendance of private theatres.

20. But Wallace denies that sitting on the stage "annoyed

the actors and disturbed the play" and asserts that the "stage was specially adapted, fitted and reserved" for spectators on the stage. He does not, however, present any evidence (Wallace 1908: 143).

21. All possible intelligent speculation as to what these lost plays might have been like, has been done by Brawner (Brawner 1942: 51-61).

22. It is rather unfortunate that Lawrence does not expound on this point.

23. Still, Lawrence's statement that The Wars of Cyrus is the first theatre-play in blank verse, does not seem to be justified.

24. Cf. Morton Paterson's analysis of the Revels Accounts in the present volume.

25. In contrast to medieval mansions, that were in most cases definitely localized, the pavilion would be a neutral, boothlike structure that could be used for a variety of scenes throughout a production. Such a structure would seem to suit the staging requirements of the First Blackfriars Theatre (see also pp. 173-174). A.M. Nagler has presented a strong case for the use of a pavilion rather than an alcove on the stage of Elizabethan public theatres (Nagler 1958: 26-32, 45-46, 49-50).

# APPENDIX

A passage about a performance at Cambridge, 1564, from John Nichols, The Progresses and Public Processions of Queen Elizabeth. (London, 1788) v.1. pp.13-14 of section "Cambridge, 1564." (to p.160-161, above): Italics mine.

"For the hearing and playing whereof, was made, by her Highnes surveyor and at her own cost, in the body of the /King's College/ CChurch, a great stage containing the breadth of the church from one side to the other, that the chapels might serve for houses. In the length it ran two of the lower chapels full, with the pillars on a side.

"Upon the fouth wall was hanged a cloth of state, with the appurtenances and halfpath, for her Majesty.

'In the rood–loft, another stage for ladies and gentlewomen to stand on. And the two lower tables, under the said rood–loft, were greatly enlarged and rayled for the choyce officers of the Court.

"There was, before her Majesty's coming, made in King's College Hall, a great stage. But, because it was judged by divers to be too little and too close for her Highness and her company, and also far from her lodging, it was taken down.

"... the Lord Chamberlayn with Mr. Secretary cam in; ... and would not suffer any to stand upon the stage, save a very few upon the north side. And the guard stood upon the ground, by the stage side, holding their lights. From the quire door unto the large stage was made as 'twere a bridge rayled no both sides; for the Queen's Grace to go to the stage: which was straightly kept."

# BIBLIOGRAPHY

| | |
|---|---|
| C. Adams 1942. | John Cranford Adams. THE GLOBE PLAYHOUSE, ITS DESIGN AND EQUIPMENT. Cambridge (Mass.) 1942. |
| C. Adams 1948 | John Cranford Adams. "The Original Staging of King Lear," Joseph Quincy Adams: MEMORIAL STUDIES. 1948. |
| Q. Adams 1911. | Joseph Quincy Adams. "The Four Pictorial Representations of the Elizabethan Stage," Journal of English and Germanic Philology, X (April, 1911) 329. |
| Q. Adams 1917. | Joseph Quincy Adams. SHAKESPEAREAN PLAYHOUSES. Boston, 1917. |
| Q. Adams 1917b. | Joseph Q. Adams. "The Conventual Buildings of the Blackfriars, London, and the Playhouses Constructed therein," Studies in Philology, 1917. |
| Q. Adams 1923. | Joseph Quincy Adams. A LIFE OF WILLIAM SHAKESPEARE. Boston, 1923. |
| Albright 1909. | Victor E. Albright. THE SHAKESPEARIAN STAGE. New York, 1909. |
| Archer 1907. | William Archer. "The Fortune Theatre 1600," Shakespeare Jahrbuch XLIV (1908), 159-166. (From the London Tribune, Oct. 12, 1907.) |
| Arkwright 1913-14. | G. E. P. Arkwright. "Elizabethan Choirboy Plays and their Music," Proceedings of the Musical Association. London, 1913-14. |

Athenaeum 1912.   "Drama section" of Athenaeum Nov. 2, 9, 23, 30, 1912; Jan. 4, 11, 18, 1913.

Baker 1907.   George Pierce Baker. THE DEVELOP-MENT OF SHAKESPEARE AS A DRAMA-TIST. New York, 1907.

Bald 1952.   R. C. Bald. "The Entrance to the Eliza-bethan Theatre," Shakespeare Quarterly III (Jan. 1952), 17-20.

Baskerville 1911.   C. R. Baskerville. "The Custom of Sitting on the Elizabethan Stage," Modern Philo-logy, VIII (1911).

Beckerman 1953.   Bernard Beckerman. "The Globe Play-house at Hofstra College, II: Notes on Reconstruction," Educational Theatre Journal V (1953), 6-11.

Beckwith 1929.   Ada Beckwith. "A Typical Elizabethan Playhouse," [drawing], Shakespeare Association Bulletin IV (Jan. 1929). Inside back cover.

Bernheimer 1958.   Richard Bernheimer. "Another Globe Theatre," Shakespeare Quarterly 9 (1958), 19-28.

Besant 1904.   Walter Besant. LONDON IN THE TIME OF THE TUDORS. London, 1904.

Blomfield 1897.   Reginald Blomfield. A HISTORY OF RENAISSANCE ARCHITECTURE IN ENGLAND, 1500-1800. 2 vols. London, 1897.

# BIBLIOGRAPHY

Braines        [W. W. Braines] THE SITE OF THE
1921.          GLOBE PLAYHOUSE SOUTHWARK.
               London, 1921.

Brawner        J. B. Brawner. THE WARS OF CYRUS:
1942.          An Early Classical Narrative Drama of
               the Child Actors. Urbana, 1942.

Brodmeier      Cecil Brodmeier. DIE SHAKESPEARE-
1904.          BÜHNE NACH DEN ALTEN BÜHNEN-
               WEISUNGEN. 1904.

Campbell       Lily Bess Campbell. SCENES AND
1923.          MACHINES ON THE ENGLISH STAGE
               DURING THE RENAISSANCE. Cam-
               bridge, 1923.

Chambers       E. K. Chambers. THE ELIZABETHAN
1923.          STAGE. 4 vols. Oxford, 1923.

Chambers       E. K. Chambers. SHAKESPEARIAN
1944.          GLEANINGS. London, 1944.

Corbin         John Corbin. "Shakespeare and the
1906.          Plastic Stage," Atlantic Monthly XCVII
               (1906), 369-383.

Corbin         John Corbin. "Shakespeare His Own
1911.          Stage-Manager," Century Magazine,
               Dec. 1911, 260-270.

D. N. B.       John A. Fuller-Maitland. "R. Farrant"
               in Dictionary of National Biography.
               vol. 6, (pp. 1091-1092) London.

Durand         W. Y. Durand. "Palaemon and Arcyte,
1905           Progne, Marcus Geminus, and the theatre

in which they were acted as described by
John Bereblock (1566)," PMLA XX (1905).

Documents
1908

DOCUMENTS RELATING TO THE OFFICE
OF THE REVELS IN THE TIME OF QUEEN
ELIZABETH, ed. Albert Feuillerat. Lou-
vain, 1908.

Feuillerat
1910.

Albert Feuillerat. LE BUREAU DES
MENUS PLAISIRS. Louvain, 1910.

Feuillerat
1910a.

Albert Feuillerat. "Quelques documents
nouveaux sur le Théâtre de Blackfriars,"
Melanges Litteraires publiés par la Faculté
des Lettres de Clermont-Ferrand. (Clermont-Ferrand, 1910).

Feuillerat
1912.

Albert Feuillerat. "The Origin of Shakespeare's Blackfriars Theatre. Recent
discovery of documents," Jahrbuch der
Deutschen Shakespeare-Gesellschaft.
Jahrgang 48. Berlin, 1912.

Feuillerat
1913.

Albert Feuillerat ed. BLACKFRIARS
RECORDS. Malone Society Reprints.
Oxford, 1913.

Flatter
1951.

Richard Flatter. "Outer, Inner, or Upper
Stage?" Shakespeare Quarterly II (1951)
171.

Folger
London 1935.

SHAKESPEARE"S LONDON. The Folger
Shakespeare Library Prints. Washington,
1935.

Folger
Theatre 1935.

THE SHAKESPEARIAN THEATRE. The
Folger Shakespeare Library Prints.
Washington, 1935.

# BIBLIOGRAPHY

Forestier       A. Forestier. "The Globe Theatre,"
1910.           [drawing] Illustrated London News, March
                19, 1910, 423.

Forestier       A. Forestier. "The Fortune Theatre,"
1911.           [drawing] Illustrated London News, Aug.
                12, 1911, 276-277.

Forrest         G. Topham Forrest. "The Architecture
1921.           of the First Globe Theatre," London
                County Council, THE SITE OF THE GLOBE
                PLAYHOUSE, Southwark. London, 1921.

Förster         Max Förster. "Altenglische Bühenrekon-
1916.           strucktionen von 1836," Shakespeare
                Jahrbuch 52 (1916). 189-190.

Gosson          Stephen Gosson. Plays Confuted in Five
1582.           Actions. (1582) in W.C. Hazlitt. THE
                ENGLISH DRAMA AND STAGE, 1543-1664.
                London, 1869. (pp. 159-218).

Granville-      H. Granville-Barker and G. B. Harrison,
Barker 1934.    eds. A COMPANION TO SHAKESPEARE
                STUDIES. Cambridge, 1934.

Graves          T. S. Graves. "A Note on the Swan Thea-
1911.           tre," Modern Philology, IX (1911-1912).

Graves          Thornton Graves. THE COURT AND THE
1913.           LONDON THEATRES DURING THE REIGN
                OF ELIZABETH. Menasha, Wisconsin,
                1913.

Graves          T. S. Graves. "The Origin of the Custom
1914.           of Sitting on the Stage," Journal of Eng-
                lish and Germanic Philology XIII (1914)

# BIBLIOGRAPHY

Griffin
1956.

Alice Griffin. "New Trends in American Theatre," Perspectives USA, 14 (1956), 130-146.

Halliday
1956.

F. E. Halliday. SHAKESPEARE: A PICTORIAL BIOGRAPHY. London, 1956.

Harbage
1941.

Alfred Harbage. SHAKESPEARE'S AUDIENCE. New York, 1941.

Harbage
1952.

Alfred Harbage. SHAKESPEARE AND THE RIVAL TRADITIONS. New York, 1952.

Harding
1954.

Davis P. Harding. "Shakespeare the Elizabethan," SHAKESPEARE: OF AN AGE AND FOR ALL TIME, Charles T. Prouty, ed. Hamden, Conn., 1954. 13-32.

Hillebrand
1926.

H. N. Hillebrand. THE CHILD ACTORS: A CHAPTER IN ELIZABETHAN STAGE HISTORY. Urbana, 1926.

Hind
1922.

A. M. Hind. WENCESLAUS HOLLAR AND HIS VIEWS OF LONDON AND WINDSOR IN THE SEVENTEENTH CENTURY. London, 1922.

Hodges
1947.

C. Walter Hodges. "The Globe Playhouse. Some Notes on a New Reconstruction," Theatre Notebook I (1947), 108-111.

Hodges
1948.

C. Walter Hodges. SHAKESPEARE AND THE PLAYERS. London, 1948.

Hodges
1950.

C. Walter Hodges. "Unworthy Scaffolds," Shakespeare Survey, 3 (1950), 83-94.

# BIBLIOGRAPHY

Hodges
1951.

C. Walter Hodges. "De Witt Again,"
Theatre Notebook, V (1951), 97-100.

Hodges
1953.

C. Walter Hodges. THE GLOBE RE-
STORED. London, 1953.

Hodges
1959.

C. Walter Hodges. "The Lantern of Taste,"
Shakespeare Survey, 12 (1959) 8-14.

Holmes
1956.

M. Holmes. "A New Theory about the
Swan Drawing," Theatre Notebook, 10
(1956), 80-83.

Hosley
1957.

Richard Hosley. "The Gallery over the
Stage in the Public Playhouse of Shake-
speare's Time," Shakespeare Quarterly,
VIII (1957), 15-31.

Hosley
1959.

Richard Hosley. "The Discovery Space
in Shakespeare's Globe," Shakespeare
Survey, 12 (1959), 35-46.

Hotson
1949.

Leslie Hotson. SHAKESPEARE'S SON-
NETS DATED AND OTHER ESSAYS. London, 1949.

Hotson
1953.

Leslie Hotson. "Shakespeare's Arena,"
Sewanee Review, LXI (1953), 347-361.

Hotson
1954.

Leslie Hotson. THE FIRST NIGHT OF
TWELFTH NIGHT. London, 1954.

Hotson
1960.

Leslie Hotson. SHAKESPEARE'S WOODEN
O. New York, 1960.

Hubbard
1923.

George Hubbard. ON THE SITE OF THE
GLOBE PLAYHOUSE OF SHAKESPEARE.
Cambridge, 1923.

# BIBLIOGRAPHY

Kernodle
1944.

George R. Kernodle. FROM ART TO
THEATRE: FORM AND CONVENTION IN
THE RENAISSANCE. Chicago, 1944.

Kernodle
1959.

George R. Kernodle. "The Open Stage:
Elizabethan or Existentialist?" Shakespeare Survey, 12 (1959), 1-7.

Lawrence
1912.

W. J. Lawrence. THE ELIZABETHAN
PLAYHOUSE AND OTHER STUDIES.
Stratford-Upon-Avon, 1912.

Lawrence
1921.

W. J. Lawrence. "The Earliest Private
Theatre Play," Times Literary Supplement. Aug. 11, 1921.

Lawrence
1927.

W. J. Lawrence. THE PHYSICAL CON-
DITIONS OF THE LONDON PUBLIC PLAY-
HOUSE. Cambridge (Mass.) 1927.

Lawrence
1930.

W. J. Lawrence. "The Elizabethan Private Playhouse," The Criterion (London)
Apr. 1930.

Lawrence
1935.

W. J. Lawrence. THOSE NUT-CRACKING
ELIZABETHANS. London, 1935.

Leacroft
1958.

Helen and Richard Leacroft. THE THEA-
TRE. London, 1958.

Lyly
1902.

John Lyly. THE COMPLETE WORKS, ed.
R. Warwick Bond. Oxford, 1902.

Miller
1959.

William E. Miller, "Periaktoi in the old
Blackfriars," Modern Language Notes,
January, 1959.

# BIBLIOGRAPHY

McMullan        Frank McMullan. "Producing Shakespeare,"
1954.           SHAKESPEARE: OF AN AGE AND FOR
                ALL TIME., ed. Charles Tyler Prouty.
                Hamden Conn., 1954.

Nagler          A.M.Nagler, ed. SOURCES OF THEAT-
1952.           RICAL HISTORY. New York, 1952.

Nagler          A.M. Nagler. "Shakespeare's Arena
1956.           Demolished," Shakespeare Newsletter, 6
                (1956), 7.

Nagler          A.M. Nagler. SHAKESPEARE'S STAGE.
1958.           New Haven, 1958.

Nagler          A.M. Nagler. "Theaterfeste der Medici,"
1960.           Maske und Kothurn VI, (1960), Heft 2.

Nagler          A.M. Nagler. "Atorno Atorno," Times
1960a.          Literary Supplement, May 6, 1960, 289.

Nichols         John Nichols. THE PROGRESSES AND
1788.           PUBLIC PROCESSIONS OF QUEEN ELIZ-
                ABETH. London, 1788.

Nicoll          Allardyce Nicoll. THE DEVELOPMENT
1927.           OF THE THEATRE. New York, 1927.

Nicoll          Allardyce Nicoll. MASKS MIMES AND
1931.           MIRACLES. New York, 1931.

Nicoll          Allardyce Nicoll. "Passing over the Stage,"
1959.           Shakespeare Survey, 12 (1959), 47-55.

Norris          Herbert Norris. COSTUME AND FASH-
1938.           ION. London, 1938.

# BIBLIOGRAPHY

Oliphant
1929.

E. H. C. Oliphant. SHAKESPEARE AND HIS
FELLOW DRAMATISTS. New York, 1929.

Peele
1910.

George Peele. THE ARRAIGNMENT OF
PARIS. Malone Society Reprints, Oxford, 1910.

Platter
1929.

Thomas Platter. ENGLANDFAHRT IM
JAHRE 1599, ed. Hans Hecht. Halle, 1929.

Prouty
1953.

Charles Tyler Prouty. "An Early Elizabethan Playhouse," Shakespeare Survey 6
(1953). 64-74.

Puttenham
1589.

George Puttenham. THE ARTE OF
ENGLISH POESIE. (1589) English Reprints, London, 1869.

Quennell
1919.

Marjorie and C. H. B. Quennell. A HIS-
TORY OF EVERYDAY THINGS IN ENG-
LAND. 2 vols. London, 1919.

Rapp
1944.

Franz Rapp. "Notes on little known materials for the history of the theatre,"
Theatre Annual, 1944.

Reynolds
1940.

George R. Reynolds. THE STAGING OF
ELIZABETHAN PLAYS AT THE RED BULL
THEATRE, 1605-1625. New York, 1940.

Reynolds
1951.

George F. Reynolds. "Was There a
'Tarras' in Shakespeare's Globe?"
Shakespeare Survey 4 (1951), 97-100.

Richardson
1837.

C. J. Richardson. SPECIMENS OF THE
ARCHITECTURE OF THE REIGNS OF
QUEEN ELIZABETH AND KING JAMES
Ist. London, 1837.

# BIBLIOGRAPHY

Rothwell
1953.

William F. Rothwell. STAGING METHODS
IN THE ENGLISH THEATRE 1550-1598.
Unpublished diss., Yale, 1953.

Rothwell
1959.

W. F. Rothwell. "Was there a Typical
Elizabethan Stage?" Shakespeare Survey,
12 (1959), 15-21.

Salter
1955.

F. M. Salter. MEDIEVAL DRAMA IN
CHESTER. Toronto, 1955.

Saunders
1960.

J. W. Saunders. "Staging at the Globe,
1599-1613," Shakespeare Quarterly XI
(1960), 401-425.

Schanzer
1956

Ernest Schanzer. "Thomas Platter's Observations on the Elizabethan Stage,"
Notes and Queries. Nov. 1956, 465-467.

Shapiro
1948.

I. A. Shapiro. "The Bankside Theatres:
Early Engravings," Shakespeare Survey,
1 (1948), 25-37.

Shapiro
1949.

I. A. Shapiro. "An Original Drawing of
the Globe Theatre," Shakespeare Survey,
2 (1949), 21-23.

Small
1935.

G. W. Small. "Shakespeare's Stage,"
Shakespeare Association Bulletin X (Jan.
1935). 31-35.

I. Smith
1956.

Irwin Smith. SHAKESPEARE'S GLOBE
PLAYHOUSE. A MODERN RECONSTRUC-
TION. New York, 1956.

M. Smith
1931.

Milton Smith. "Shakespeare in the Schools,"
Shakespeare Association Bulletin VI
(April 1931). 38-47.

# BIBLIOGRAPHY

| | |
|---|---|
| Southern 1951. | Richard Southern. CHANGEABLE SCENERY. London, 1951. |
| Southern 1959. | Richard Southern. "On Reconstructing a Practicable Elizabethan Public Playhouse," Shakespeare Survey, 12 (1959), 22-34. |
| Stopes 1910. | C. C. Stopes. WILLIAM HUNNIS AND THE REVELS OF THE CHAPEL ROYAL: A STUDY OF HIS PERIOD AND THE INFLUENCE WHICH AFFECTED SHAKESPEARE. Louvin, 1910. |
| Summerson 1953. | John Summerson. ARCHITECTURE IN BRITAIN 1530 to 1830. London, 1953. |
| Thorndike 1916. | A. H. Thorndike. SHAKESPEARE'S THEATRE. New York, 1916. |
| Wallace 1908. | Charles W. Wallace. THE CHILDREN OF THE CHAPEL AT BLACKFRIARS. Univ. of Nebraska, 1908. |
| Wallace 1912. | Charles W. Wallace. THE EVOLUTION OF THE ENGLISH DRAMA UP TO SHAKESPEARE WITH A HISTORY OF THE FIRST BLACKFRIARS THEATRE. vol. 4, Schriften der Deutschen Shakespeare Gesellschaft, Berlin, 1912. |
| Wickham 1959. | Glynne Wickham. EARLY ENGLISH STAGES. 2 vols. London, 1959- |
| Wilson 1953. | F. P. Wilson. "The Elizabethan Theatre," Neophilologus, XXXIX (1953), 40-58. |

# INDEX

191

# INDEX

Italian ladies, 24
Italian language, 50
Italian mannerist architects, 81
Italian players, 7, 11, 12
Iuno, 169

Jacobethan style, 81
Johnson & Steevens Shakespeare, 61, 112
Jones, Inigo, 81, 172
Jonson, Ben, 176

Keller, Dr. Wolfgang, 165
Kenilworth, 148
Kernodle, George R., 61, 62, 78, 81-82, 83, 114, 117
King Lear, 79, 89
King's College, 38
King's Men, 76
Knight of the Burning Rock, The, 34
Ladies Mask, 11
Lanceknights Mask, 11
Lane, Sir Robert, 7
Latin language, 49, 50
Lawrence, W. J., 56, 112, 146, 157-159, 162-163, 165, 176, 177
Leicester, Earl of, 7, 11, 149, 151
Lent, 12
Libanio, 168
Lincoln's Inn, 148
Lodge, Thomas, 140
London, Maps and views of, 56, 57, 60, 67

London Topographical Society, The, 91, 116
Lord Admiral, 7
Lord Chamberlain, 5, 7, 8
Lord Treasurer, 49
Loseley MSS, 139, 174
Low Countries, 85
Lyly, John, 139-140, 151-155, 160, 164-166, 174

Macbeth, 100
Mad World My Masters, A, 176
Maids of Honor, 49
Malcontent, The, 176
Malone, Edmund, 61, 112
Mamillia, 11
Marlowe, Christopher, 140, 166
Marston, John, 176
Mask of Astronomers, 25
Mask of Barbarians, 25
Mask of Fishermen, 42
Mask of Mariners, 18
Mask of Musicians, 42, 52
Master of the Children, 141, 176. See also Bower, Edwards, Farrant, Hunnis
Master of the Revels, 5, 8, 9, 13, 25, 33, 52, 144
Merchant Tailors, Children of, 7, 11
Mercury, 40
Michelangelo, 80
Middleton, John, 176
Mileta, 170-171
Miller, William E., 171-172, 174
Montemayor, 20
Montmorency, Duc de, 8, 12, 35